# HISTORY ON THE G

*Photo*. D. D. Griffiths.

Alfred John Bird, N.D.A., F.S.A. 1909—1976.

# HISTORY ON THE GROUND

An Inventory of unrecorded material relating to the Mid-Anglo-Welsh
Borderland, with Introductory Chapters

by

## A. J. BIRD
F.S.A.

UNIVERSITY OF WALES PRESS
1977

© UNIVERSITY OF WALES PRESS, 1977

ISBN O 7083 0627 6

PRINTED IN WALES
BY THE CAMBRIAN NEWS (ABERYSTWYTH) LTD.

for

Phyllis, Carol

and

Helen Jane

# CONTENTS

# FOREWORD

## by

## Emeritus Professor E. G. Bowen, M.A., D.Litt., Ll.D., F.S.A.

IN these days, when the study of the environment looms so large in both academic and non-academic fields, any material that contributes to additional interest in, or knowledge of the past must be welcomed. Masses of material have been gathered in Britain over the years, and remain either unsorted or recorded on cards hidden away in official filing cabinets. One of the most important of such collections in the archaeological field is, for example, the Catalogue of Bronze Age Implements for Britain, initiated many years ago by Miss Lily F. Chitty, F.S.A., and destined for the British Museum. This gives the location of every Bronze Age find, a drawing or photograph of the implement in question, the literature available concerning it, and in which museum the object or objects in question may be seen by members of the public. Closely allied to this catalogue, but covering a very much wider field, is a card index of local antiquities not recorded on the Ordnance Survey maps, but including sites of importance ranging from the Palaeolithic to Modern Times, now in possession of the Ordnance Survey. Most of this material has been collected by amateur local correspondents of the Survey over the years, including this work by Mr. A. J. Bird, who has acted as such a correspondent. It has been decided to publish his relevant records for the Clun area on the Anglo-Welsh Borderland in the form of an Inventory accompanied by chapters related to this material. It is hoped that this publication, the first of its kind yet attempted, will be of interest, not only to students, but to the general public who are becoming increasingly aware of the treasures that lie partly hidden and forgotten in our rich inheritance in Britain.

In many ways, this type of work is reminiscent of that commissioned by the Ordnance Survey and undertaken in the early 19th. century by John O'Donovan (1809-1861). He was the son of a Kilkenny farmer, and claimed descent from Oilliol Oluim, King of Munster. Inheriting a flair for ancient Irish history and folk culture, he obtained work in the Irish Record Office in 1826, and three years later joined the historical department of the Ordnance Survey of Ireland. O'Donovan was not too pleased with his remuneration for this appointment, as he refers to it as 'a very small stipend, which I accepted after some hesitation'. Nevertheless, he visited every part of Ireland, assembling an incredible mass of notes on archaeology, history, traditions and the etymology of place-names, in many MSS which are now preseved in the Royal Irish Academy in Dublin. His was an achievement of the greatest importance, and is mentioned here merely to illustrate the possibilities which derive from painstaking fieldwork, recording and personal contacts. While the present work on the Welsh Marches does not pretend to emulate O'Donovan's work, the methods and techniques applied have much in common. Altogether, some seventy new records were obtained each year in the mid-Borderland, which may be the basis for some satisfaction, as A. J. Bird worked, unlike O'Donovan, on a part-time voluntary system over a period of twenty-five years.

## NOTE

Unfortunately, Mr. Bird died suddenly as this work was going through the press and proof reading has in consequence to be undertaken by others. I had the great advantage of co-operating closely with the author in the preparation of the original text and in this way of being thoroughly familiar with the subject matter. All that has been undertaken is the correction of the obvious, and for the most part, of purely verbal errors. The work of proof reading has been made possible by the kind assistance rendered by Mr. and Mrs. Carl Chadwick, close friends and admirers of the author. We are sure that Mr. Bird would have wished me to thank them, the Printers, and the Director and officers of the University of Wales Press for their courtesy, guidance and consideration at all times in the production of this book.

E. G. Bowen.

1st May, 1976.

# ACKNOWLEDGEMENTS

The fieldwork undertaken since 1945 covered hundreds of square miles, involving long distances on foot, so that many local people could be interviewed. They are too numerous to mention individually, but everywhere they offered their kindness, interest and hospitality in boundless measure, from teenagers to octogenarians, and it is they who deserve our deep thanks and appreciation for the contributions which they made. Grateful reference, in particular, should be made to the number of close friends who have since passed on: Professor D. R. Dudley, Miss H. Auden, Mrs. Lilian Hayward, Tom Hamar, H. C. Jones, L. C. Lloyd, W. J. Slack and F. Lavender—who all gave invaluable assistance. My own family, Mrs. K. M. Bird, and both sons, Julian and Christopher, from very early ages, displayed the deepest interest in all the fieldwork; without their efforts, the scope of the work would not have attained such proportions, which averaged one new find at least each week. Invaluable advice and encouragement also was extended throughout by C. W. Phillips, Archaeological Officer of the Ordnance Survey, and by Miss Lily F. Chitty who fortunately lived quite near, and was ever ready with her vast resources of information and expertise to express considered opinions and to offer suggestions, particularly while on the numerous inspection tours she made with us in the field. I am also indebted to Dr. Desmond Slay, of the English Dept. U.C.W., Aberystwyth, for advice on place names. Finally, grateful appreciation in the fullest measure must be accorded to Emeritus Professor E. G. Bowen, who has closely watched the work unfold over the greater part of the time, and who has devoted much time and unstinted energy to assembling the material into a form which is readily available to the reader for any extension of the fieldwork over the Principality.

I acknowledge also the expert advice and assistance willingly given by my colleagues in the Department of Geography, University College of Wales, Aberystwyth, particularly to Mr. Morlais Hughes and Mr. Edward James for cartography, and to Mr. David Griffiths for photography.

# SELECTED BIBLIOGRAPHY

*Antiquity*

*Archaeologia Cambrensis*

Atkinson, R. C., *'Field Archaeology'*, Methuen, 1946.
Auden, J. E., *'Shropshire'*, Methuen, 1932.
Braun, H. S., *'The English Castle'*, Batsford, 1936.
British Museum Guide to the Antiquities of the Stone Age, 1921.
   ,,       ,,     ,,     ,,     ,,    ,, ,, Bronze Age, 1920.
   ,,       ,,     ,,     ,,     ,,    ,, ,, Early Iron Age, 1921.
   ,,       ,,     ,,     ,, Greek & Roman Life, 1920.

*Bulletin of the Board of Celtic Studies.*
Caradoc & Severn Valley Field Club, *'Record of Bare Facts'* (Annual vols.).
Chitty, Lily F., *'The Clun-Clee Ridgeway'* (Culture & Environment. Essays in honour of Sir Cyril Fox), Kegan Paul, 1963.
Clark, Grahame, *'Prehistoric England'*, Batsford, 1940.
Donkin, R. A., *'The Cistercian Order in Medieval England; some conclusions'*. Inst. of British Geographers Trans. & Papers, 1963, no. 33, pp. 181-198.
Fleure, H. J. & Davies, M., *'Natural History of Man in Britain'*. Collins, 1971
Foster, I. Ll. & Daniel, Glyn. *'Prehistoric & Early Wales'*, Routledge & Kegan Paul, 1965.
Fox, Sir Cyril, *'Offa's Dyke'*. Oxford Univ. Press, 1955 for British Academy.
Fox, Sir Cyril, *'The Personality of Britain'*. Cardiff, Nat. Mus. of Wales, 1952.
Gazetteer of Welsh Place-names (Rhestr o Enwau Lleoedd), ed. Elwyn Davies, Cardiff, Univ. Wales Press, 1967.
Grimes, W. F., *'The Prehistory of Wales'*, 1951, a guide to the collection in the National Museum of Wales, Cardiff.
Hawkes, J. *'A Guide to the Prehistoric & Roman Monuments of England & Wales'*. 1951.
Hawkes, J. & C. F. C. *'Prehistoric Britain'*, Penguin, 1958.
Hawkins, G. S., *'Stonehenge Decoded'*, Fontana, London, 5th. impression, 1974.
Jones, Francis, *'Holy Wells of Wales'*, Cardiff, Univ. Wales Press, 1954.
Jones, H. C., *'The South-west Borderland of Shropshire'*. Shrewsbury, 1938, pp. 37-81.
    Also special contributions to *Car. & Sev. Vall. E. C. Record of Bare Facts* 1932-40, vol. ix pp. 65-71, pp. 71-73, pp. 188-198, pp. 263-267, vol. x pp. 74-80, vol. xi pp. 126-131.
Jones, P. Thoresby, *'Welsh Border Country'*, Batsford, 1938.

Montgomery Collections.

Nash-Williams, V. E., 'The Roman Frontier in Wales'. Cardiff, Univ. Wales Press, 1954, & 2nd. revd. edn. by Jarrett, M. G. 1969.

Nash-Williams, V. E., 'Early Christian Monuments of Wales', Cardiff, Univ. Wales Press, 1950 for the National Museum of Wales.

Oakley, Kenneth P., 'Man the Tool-maker'. Brit. Mus. Nat. Hist. 1956. 3rd Edit.

Ordnance Survey series of historical maps, e.g. Roman Britain, Britain in the Iron Age, Monastic Britain, Ancient Britain etc.

Ordnance Survey, Professional Papers no. 13, new series, Field Archaeology. H.M.S.O., 1963 (4th edn.) & subsequent.

Piggott, S. 'British Prehistory', 1949.

Quennell, M. & C.H.B., 'Everyday Things in England 1066-1499'. Batsford, 1931.

Richards, Melville. Welsh Administrative and Territorial Units. Cardiff Univ. Wales Press. 1969.

Richmond, I. A., 'Roman Britain', Pelican 1963.

Royal Commission on Ancient Monuments, Wales. County Inventories for Radnorshire and Montgomeryshire.

Saunders, Roy. 'The Drovers' Highway', Oldbourne, 1959.

Shotton, F. W., Chitty, Lily F. & Seaby, W. A. 'A new centre of Stone Axe Dispersal on the Welsh Border'. Proc. Prehistoric Socy. 1951, pp. 159-167.

Shotton, F. W. 'New Petrological Groups Based on Axes from the West Midlands'. Proc. Prehistoric Socy. xxv, 1959, pp. 135-143.

Shropshire Archaeological Society. Transactions.

Slack, W. J. 'The Shropshire Hearth Tax Roll of 1672'. Shropshire Archaeological and Parish Register Society, 1949.

Thom, A., Megalithic Lunar Observatories, Oxford 1971.

Townships of Clun Enclosure Award, 1836, unpublished MSS in Clun Museum.

Webster, G. & Dudley, D. R. 'The Roman Conquest of Britain'. London, 1965.

Wheeler, Sir R. E. M., 'Prehistoric & Roman Wales'. Oxford, 1925.

Wood, Eric S. 'Field Guide to Archaeology in Britain'. Collins, 1963.

Although the R.C.A.M. Inventories are referred to above, it should be appreciated that those which are relevant to the area are some 50 years or more old, and did not at the time include material beyond mediaeval times. This survey, therefore, apart from plotting informative material unrecorded on the O.S. maps, as stated in the terms of reference, records many changes that have taken place since the original compilation of these Inventories, and antedates the extension of the recording of items by the R.C.A.M. up to more recent times to include Industrial Archaeology, a decision taken some four years ago.

## Chapter I

# ARCHAEOLOGY AND THE ORDNANCE SURVEY

It is well-known that the Ordnance Survey of Great Britain is unique among National Surveys in its long-established practice of showing antiquities in detail on its maps of all scales. There is no doubt that the original inspiration for this goes back to General Roy in the 18th century, who was so closely associated with the founding of the Survey. Roy was one of the most distinguished archaeologists of his time, and particularly interested in Roman military sites in Scotland. As various editions of Ordnance Survey maps appeared, more and more attention was paid to the accurate showing of antiquities, and in this way a great mass of material found its way onto the maps by the close of the 19th century. There remained, however, a serious weakness in the fact that the Survey did not possess a professional archaeologist capable of checking the mass of information taken up by the surveyors in the field, nor was any provision made for the examination of areas where local information was wanting. The dawn of the 20th century, however, saw the rise of Archaeology into a scientific study in its own right, and during the first fifty years of the new century, enormous progress was made as a result of scientifically conducted excavations, and the teaching of the subject at university level. Public demand in the present century, furthermore, has been instrumental in encouraging the production of Period Maps, and today the list of such publications is impressive:

Roman Britain 1st edn. 1924.
Roman Britain 2nd edn. 1928.
XVIIth Century Britain, 1930.
Neolithic Wessex, 1932.
Map of the Trent Basin (Neolithic), 1933.
Celtic Earthworks of Salisbury Plain, 1933.
Britain in the Dark Ages (South sheet), 1935.
Neolithic South Wales, 1936.
Britain in the Dark Ages (North sheet), 1938.
Monastic Britain, 1950.
Ancient Britain, 1951.
Monastic Britain, 1954 and 1955.

Southern Britain in the Iron Age, 1962.
Hadrian's Wall, 1963.
Map of Britain in the Dark Ages (one sheet) 1966 (text revd. 1971).
Antonine Wall, 1969.
Britain before the Norman Conquest, 1973.

Consequently, at the end of the First World War, the Ordnance Survey Office was able to appoint an Archaeology Officer, the first holder of the post being the late Dr. O. G. S. Crawford, C.B.E., Litt.D., F.B.A. He was responsible for advising the Director-General on all archaeological matters relating to the Survey's work, which in practice made him responsible for the revision of antiquities. Dr. Crawford's tenure of office lasted until the beginning of the Second World War when the work of the Survey was once again disturbed. When the archaeological Division of the Survey was revived in 1947, it was confronted with the difficulty of keeping track of all the day-to-day archaeological happenings throughout the country, so great had been the growth of interest in the subject. Dr. Crawford had made a beginning in attempting to deal with this problem by the organization of an auxiliary system of honorary correspondents, and this has been revised and considerably expanded under Dr. Crawford's successor, Mr. C. W. Phillips, M.A., O.B.E., F.S.A., With the aid of honorary correspondents a great deal of information continued to be gathered and put on record. In its *Notes for Correspondents of the Archaeology Division,* published in 1958, a distiction is made between what is already recorded in the form of clearly visible monuments, such as megalithic tombs, hill-forts, or Norman castles, and the smaller material not recorded. The directions specifically state that local correspondents must direct their attention to the importance of recording small finds. The discovery of a single sherd of pottery or a coin may be the clue to an important new site. Even where a small find has no sequel of this kind, a good record of such finds helps to build up our knowledge of the distribution of given cultures or phrases of life over the country as a whole. A case in point would be the careful recovering of small flint implements turned up casually by ploughing, or even by rabbits or moles. Many of these may be too insignificant or too ill-authenticated to find their way onto printed maps, but information about them is placed in the records of the Archaeological Division and corrections are at once made (e.g. tumulus to motte.) Find spots of portable objects found on the surface were noted by the symbol +, or if recovered stratigraphically, by Old English lettering; hitherto unrecorded visible antiquities, either undisturbed or ruinous, were marked by the + and O. E. lettering. Furthermore, it was the custom in the past to take no official notice of antiquities later in date than the Restoration Period, but today this limitation is obsolete. The later date is now brought well forward into the nineteenth century, thereby including buildings, obsolete canals, rail tracks, ironworks, foundries and much that came under the heading of Industrial Archaeology, and where the Correspondent worked in an essentially rural area, information about field systems, remains of lynchets, and particularly the trackways of the cattle drovers and their shoeing places, are equally significant, and have been recorded. This period is of special interest in that it can be studied in documents, and the results of the study related to features on the ground. In order to get the work of the honorary correspondents properly organised, they were supplied with the necessary

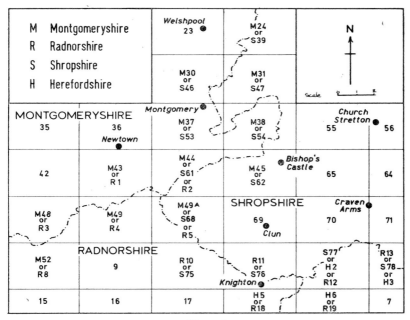

Figure 1

LOCATION INDEX

Showing the coverage of 6″ County series O.S. maps used for the study area. Each is the full sheet, and should be divided into the quadrants referred to in the Inventory. Those which overlap county boundaries bear two or more numbers as alternatives.

six-inch maps, 1/10,560 scale, to cover the area to be watched, and when the information upon them was substantial, the maps were to be returned temporarily to the Archaeological Division of the Survey, where the notes were abstracted. Each sheet could, in fact, be used as a field note-book page. The final notebook would thus consist of all the maps so used. Proof of their having been put to good use is often reflected in the mudstains, rain-spots and creases incurred in the field. Keen and conscientious recorders went further, and kept a carefully annotated card catalogue of each find recorded on the maps, and even exceeded their terms of reference by recording items known to be spurious, and much of the non-material culture with which they came into contact in their interviews. This material, as is well-known, may often be associated with lost sites of considerable historical and archaeological significance, such as stories of battles fought in the locality, and references, cryptic or suggestive, to King Arthur that have persisted at so many sites in the countryside. So important did the Ordnance Survey consider this work that the first Archaeology Officer issued a special Handbook entitled '*Field Archaeology: Some Notes for Beginners issued by the Ordnance Survey*' in 1921. This publication has been revised five times subsequently, with the fifth edition dated as recently as 1973, and covering the whole field from the Palaeolithic to the Industrial Age. Full use has been made of this book.

At this time there were about twenty-five correspondents over the five regions of England and Wales. Many areas had never been covered at close range, including, in particular, the Middle Borderland of Wales. Up to that time, the area had been invigilated by Miss Lily F. Chitty from her home at Pontesbury, and she relied upon local antiquarians to give her verbal messages, too often without precise reference to the 6″ maps. Her many excursions by public transport and attendances at field meetings were indeed commendable, and many positive records were thus obtained. But much more awaited discovery, preferably by someone living on the spot, well-known among the local population, enthusiastic enough to provide reliable recordings. I have always had a lifelong interest as an amateur in all things historical. There was always the excitement in finding something still older than hitherto. Norman work prompted one to look for Saxon remains, and Saxon in turn back to Roman, Iron Age and Stone Age. From our Nottingham home, a holiday venture at Snitton, near Ludlow in 1936 was used as a base for penetration over the Border. Arriving in Clun in pursuit of local information literature, acquaintance was made with Mr. Tom Hamar, shop-keeper and curator of the Museum there under the Clun Town Trust. He not only provided a variety of publications, but even devoted many hours to showing his collection of several thousand Stone Age flint implements, collected locally, but only recorded on 6″ maps in a general way. Having noted a likely spot which could be visited on the way back to Ludlow, three flint scrapers were found at Brandhill, which he later confirmed as genuine. This initial experience opened up a new field of interest, antedating earlier discoveries by anything up to two thousand years.

Soon after returning to Nottingham, some flint implements were picked up on the surface of the ground in the garden at Stanton-on-Wolds. Local opinion prompted excavation, resulting in a major find, which has been published by the Thoroton Society. Miss Chitty was kept informed throughout, and by 1940, on moving to the Clun area, we were collecting and recording flints in such numbers that visits to Pontesbury were becoming too frequent to enter the many finds on her maps. It was at this juncture in 1945 that she recommended the author to the Archaeology Officer of the Ordnance Survey, Mr. C. W. Phillips, to be enrolled as one of their Honorary Correspondents. Travel and subsistence allowances were made, the work was optional, and one was free to go on journeys of one's choice in the area. In the 1960's, the O.S. found on a re-appraisal of the position that a number of correspondents were accumulating maps on which precisely nothing had been entered, and that whole areas were in consequence still completely blank. Those who had been sufficiently devoted to the work decided to continue on a voluntary basis, which the author has done to date.

The area over which work was to be undertaken was naturally not precisely defined, but it generally extended (Fig. 1) over a rectangular area from Church Stretton in Shropshire, to Knighton on the Radnorshire border, to Newtown in Montgomeryshire, overspilling into the Craven Arms area. The work was based on Clun in close association with Clun Museum as Joint Curator. It lasted over a period of fifteen years, when the author moved to western Cardiganshire, where similar recording is still continuing eastwards back to the original area.

It so happens that the area on the Welsh Borderland defined above is one through which few major roads passed, and railways served only three sides of the perimeter. It was essentially rural and sparsely populated, and in many ways its historical monuments, except for the more obvious ones, have been much neglected. In this way, therefore, there was much to be recorded. With the encouragement of the Ordnance Survey Department, and many distinguished archaeologists and friends in Britain and in our local and National Institutions, it has now been decided to publish the recordings so made in the Borderland area. Such is the origin of this work. It was obvious that the inventory should be placed on record for future workers, and this forms the basis of this volume. At the same time, it was equally obvious that an Inventory of this nature, published by itself, would have little appeal to the general reader, so the chapters which precede it are an attempt to record the activities of an Honorary Correspondent in such varied rôles as a Stone Age flint collector, a surveyor of Megalithic monuments, an inspector of recorded hill-forts, a visitor to old churches and churchyards, and a traveller over pre-historic trackways, border dykes and the drover roads of later times. The greatly increased public interest in archaeology and in all memorials of the past is accompanied today by an increased interest in the environment as a whole.


CHAPTER II

## WHAT THE LAND SURFACE HAS TO TELL

A BRIEF reference to the relief features of the Central Welsh Borderland should be made at the outset. Indeed, as will be shown later, this aspect of the Borderland can be shown to have had a relevant bearing on the siting of antiquities.

On the eastern boundary of the area, west of the Ludlow to Church Stretton A49 road, the land rises from about 400 feet (122 m.) above O.D. to around 1,600 feet (487 m), forming a series of peneplains intersected by river systems. Generally speaking, the land surface which presents itself to us today consists of three main types.

Firstly, the valley floors so formed by the river systems are of fertile alluvium, liable to seasonal flooding generally of short duration. Secondly where the land rises to form the hill-slopes, an appreciable programme of land development has been maintained, due to the progress in the mechan-isation of agriculture and to the expansion of forestry in recent times. Fertil-isers have been applied to restore plant nutrition and to reduce the acidity of the soils which has resulted from the continual weathering and leeching of their virgin condition. Land which has thus been treated is carrying a heavier head of livestock than hitherto, but that which is agriculturally unremunera-tive has been disposed of to the Forestry Commission and planted with ex-tensive areas of conifers. Above this second belt of marginal land is the third where there are considerable areas of moorland and upland peat, which began to form with the increasing humidity at the close of the Bronze Age and have continued to the present time.

Areas exposed to the westerly prevailing winds, and areas facing north-wards and in consequence correspondingly sunless and prone to severe winter conditions, are two appreciable factors in archaeological fieldwork, and success in discovery depends to a great extent on the appreciation of these physical and land utilisation factors.

Geologically, the formations are Devonian (Old Red Sandstone), Silurian (Ludlow, Wenlock and Llandovery) and Ordovician (Caradoc). But the predominant and important feature is that there is no flint-bearing chalk. The only flint found naturally has been glacially transported, ochreous in colour and Irish in origin.

The earliest phases of man's existence in the Palaeolithic period do not appear to be represented in this area. If Palaeolithic Man ever existed here, the evidence in the form of artefacts lies deep down beneath the Glacial Drift overlay. Neither have any caves in the area yielded any evidence of this period, though they have done so elsewhere in the Principality, as at Paviland in the south, and, even so, all cave occupation known in Britain as a whole tends to belong to the Upper Palaeolithic merging into the Mesolithic Period. All that the field worker can do, therefore, is to watch for unrecognised caves which give promise of results, bearing in mind that the cave entrances are generally partly or wholly sealed by *detritus* which has accumulated over the years.

In terms of what the land surface has to tell regarding the Mesolithic Period which follows, one can only suggest that peat-cuttings and deep drainage channel diggings, especially near to former swampy or lacustrine areas, might offer the best possibilities. This Period is, in effect, an overlap between two ways of life—hunting and gathering food, and controlled food production. Modern thought places the Mesolithic Age as beginning around 8,000 years B.C., when the British Isles were being cut off from the European continent by the Channel break-through at Dungeness.

We can now think, in particular, of the three zones—agricultural, forests and moorland peats. In this area, major development projects are nearly all confined to agricultural activities, to the Forestry Commission and to water conservation. Arable farming has yielded the bulk of the prehistoric material, particularly in the lowest and middle zones. The reason is that unless the plough reaches the evidence below the present soil, it would normally remain at the occupational floor *in perpetuum*. Ideally, therefore, it is essential 'to follow the plough' and other agricultural machinery.

Regarding the activities of the Forestry Commission, in the middle zone chiefly, other tactics must be employed in field enquiries. Although the Commission's personnel have been highly co-operative, their *modus operandi* on the land is in some ways different from that of the agriculturalist. Being highly mechanised, their operational speed is too great to allow more than a cursory inspection. But an even more formidable obstacle is that their 'Prairie Buster' type of plough turns over a much deeper furrow, often to 17 inches (43 cm.), the result being that a flint site at the usual 6 to 11 inches (15 to 28 cm.) from the surface can be completely turned over and placed in layers deeper than the original level at which early man lived. It is only on the more shallow soils, resting on rock outcrop, that an opportunity to find anything occurs. Where features, such as tumuli and cairns, can be discerned beforehand, the Forestry Commission is careful to circumvent them. The best approach to the Forestry worker is to solicit the goodwill of the Area Forester in charge, especially if with tact one provides a little 'private tuition' on potential discoveries. Failure to do so in the past appears, in one instance, to have resulted in the loss of a collection of stone celts below the Bury Ditches hill-fort (3 m. N. of Clun). These were found when preparing the ground for planting, and although noted as curious by forestry personnel at the time, were tossed back into the furrow and re-buried. No one knows where they lie today, and it is doubtful if they will ever come to light again, at least for many years.

Water conservation, with its increasing tempo, constitutes a real threat to this kind of work. As a result of demands by major industrial areas in England, many of the deep-sided valleys are being dammed and flooded. Political considerations and natural history conservation are irrelevant to this study, but archaeologically this area, in particular, stands to lose for ever beneath the waters of the reservoirs many undetected sites of importance. It is only fair, however, to the Water Authorities to recognise that they do, in fact, undertake the most elaborate rescue operations before flooding, after consultations with the Ancient Monuments Board, as was done in the case of the Llyn Brianne Reservoir and in the Alun basin outside this study area.

The land surface can only tell one something, if one looks carefully at what it can show, ignoring the features such as hedgerows and modern intrusions into the landscape, and if one uses a little common-sense associated with an attempt to 'live in the past'. For example, in recording flint-sites, it was found that they invariably occurred on hill-slopes with a southern aspect. Again, easy access to water, whether spring or stream, was a deciding factor in the choice of habitation sites by Stone Age Man. If the available water was south of a hill, then the flint site was usually discovered on the lower slopes of that hill; but, if there was inadequate water to the south, and an available supply to the north of it, then the flint sites were located on the upper parts of that hill with a southern aspect a short distance from the summit. Having decided that a certain slope might yield a find on being ploughed, a contemplative study of the terrain, especially when low oblique sunlight formed shadows, often revealed a slight levelling-off of the contour. Sometimes these traces of original platforms were conspicuous. Otherwise, due to weathering and soil movement, they might only be detected by sighting from a kneeling position, especially if the site had been cultivated for a few seasons. Again, a hollow of a few feet diameter in the ground does not necessarily imply that one has found the floor of a primitive hut. It is more likely that a large tree has in the past been blown down in a gale, its root system removing the soil adhering to the roots in doing so and leaving the hollow; the tree remains being long since decayed and vanished. Such, then, are some of the things which the land surface has to tell us, albeit by signs, and our success depends on how we use our eyes and apply common-sense as we move over the landscape.

## Chapter III

## THE FLINT COLLECTOR IN THE FIELD

THE Neolithic Period which followed the Mesolithic, and which is thought to have had its beginning here in the 4th millennium B.C. long after its origins in the Near East, is most prolifically represented in this area. Even today, a very wide scope is offered to field observers to recognise, recover and record every piece of flint which comes to light, whether it is the finished artefact, or the waste chippings incurred in its manufacture. From their wide variety of types and from their equally wide concentrations along the margins of the network of both major and minor trackways across this zone, and even beyond, deep into Wales, it is clear that the population density hereabouts was at least appreciable and a considerable continuity of settlement is displayed, and also that trading was extensive in the necessities of life from one community to another. It would seem that the bulk of the flint in the form of crude nodules was brought along these routes from the chalk-bearing formations of Wiltshire, though a smaller percentage, generally of an ochreous colouration, found its way here from an Irish source as glacial deposits on the beaches of Cardigan Bay.

The artefacts and waste material vary in colour from pale to dark grey, due to age and extensive exposure. The longer the exposure to sunlight, the lighter becomes the outside of the flake, so that the original very dark colour of the newly-mined flint is now seen through a film of white. The thicker this film has become over the years, the lighter grey the flake appears.[1]

As is well-known, a crude nodule of flint was chipped by removing a convenient end to give a 'working platform'. By sharp, but accurate, blows with a pointed hammer-stone around the platform edge, primary flakes were struck off. As the edges of these would be too thin to be durable, so secondary flaking was done by pressure, using a fabricator to make the intended implement. At the point where the blow was struck by the pointed hammer-stone, a 'bulb of percussion' can be seen on the struck-off flake, which, of course, would leave a counter-part matrix hollow on the parent flint. Radiating from the point of percussion are seen concentric ripple rings. These are the very features which, however small, proclaim at once to the field-worker that it is almost certainly a flake struck off by human hands, and these features should be looked for immediately.

The various types of the smaller flint artefacts often bear professional descriptive names, but in simpler terms for the amateur the following is a list of the more common objects likely to be encountered :— (Figure 2)

(a)  end-scraper—used as a kind of carpenter's plane.
(b)  side-scraper.
(c)  thumb-scraper—probably used for removing fat from the inside of pelts in the process of curing for leather or clothing.
(d)  hollow-scraper—used as a spoke-shave for smoothing arrow or spear shafts to the required diameter.
(e)  engraving tools—for any piercing use, e.g. making a groove or a hole in leather for sewing with sinews.
(f)  saw-edged tools—for cutting off tidily the square ends of shafts.
(g)  knives.
(h)  scalpel-like tools—for delicate work (even suggesting surgery).

[1] This would seem to be proved by the author in a Nottinghamshire excavation in 1938 (*vide* Bird, A. J. & K. M., *A Prehistoric Hutfloor at Stanton-on-the-Wolds, Nottinghamshire*. Trans. Thoroton Soc. 1972, pp. 4-13), when the halves of a broken flint flake were found. Apparently, and for want of a better explanation, the flake had been broken accidentally by Stone Age man, the one half had been discarded and trodden deep into the floor material of the hut away from the light. The other half was flung outside, where it remained for a long time on the contemporary ground surface, and so became much paler than the other. Both halves fitted exactly with the contrasting colours meeting at the fracture.

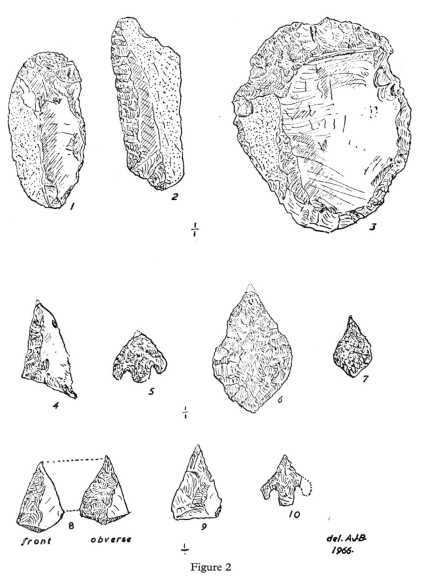

Figure 2

Examples of flint artefacts

(i)   fabricators—for pressure-flaking in implement making.

(j)   curved cutting-edged blades—for possible extraction of marrow from bones.

(k)   arrowheads.

(l)   spearheads.

Scrapers and knife blades are the most common, while arrowheads vary in form from site to site, and even on each site, from pale to dark grey, from leaf-shaped to single or double barbed, to symmetrical barbed and tanged. (Fig. 2) Stray specimens were generally of the last form. Spearheads were leaf-shaped. A less common type is known as the transverse arrowhead—approximately four centimeters long with a tang and horizontal cutting edge. This type is usually thought to have been used for shooting birds, immobilising them, if it penetrated the muscles or sinews on the underside of the wings, as the birds flew overhead. There is little doubt that the hunters were excellent marksmen. The arrow-head variants from leaf-shaped to the barbed and tanged would seem to indicate the development of improved types throughout the cultural periods. Prehistoric man found that an arrowhead, on which he had by chance left a barb, proved more vulnerable to an animal, being less likely to be extracted from the flesh than without a barb; and two barbs proved even more effective, and, by fashioning a tang, the arrowhead could the more easily and securely be fixed to the shaft. It would seem that, with the advent of the Bronze Age and the first use of metals, the flint arrowhead was still retained in use, for the obvious reason that the metal one would be more valuable than flint, especially as an arrow was more likely to be lost.

Thumb-scrapers include some very small specimens, and could even have been used by the children for dressing the skins of the smaller animals. Knife blades vary from large to very delicately refined specimens. Clun Museum possesses an exquisite set of three tools found near Brandon Camp, near Leintwardine. These comprise a small knife blade, a boring tool and a scalpel. Professor Stuart Piggott, who examined them, suggested that they could easily be a set of surgical instruments used particularly in operations on the head for the probable removal of a brain cyst, as is done today by veterinary surgeons while dealing with Gid in sheep. By using herbs as a local anaesthetic, the hair could be removed with the knife and the scalp skin cut and folded back from the area of the operation; then, by using the engraver point as a chisel, the bone could by grooving be penetrated, and a disc of the bone removed; by using the scalpel, the offending cyst could be lifted out; finally, the disc would be returned to its place in the skull, as well as the skin. It is

known that this operation was not only performed, but that it was also success-
ful, as Piggott has obtained skulls where the disc of bone has re-knitted back
to the skull. It is generally assumed that the operation was for cyst removal,
but it may well be that it was done to release an evil spirit. It could have even
been done by the counter-part of the witch doctor, who perhaps practiced
hypnosis in *lieu* of herbal anaesthetics. A local antiquary went so far as to
suggest that this particular set of tools was used by King Bran's physician.
Bran, after whom the Brandon Camp is named, was the father of Caratacus[2]
the famous leader of the Britons against the Romans.

It was always sound practice to hold each implement as it was intended, by
finding the most comfortable position, thereby assessing its suitability to a
particular use. In the manufacture of such sharp tools as flint, it was obvious
that secondary flaking would have to be carried out to a point whereby the
maximum comfort to the hand of the user would be ensured. It was found by
holding them thus that they fitted the right hand in practically every instance.
Only one specimen (in Clun Museum) is known from the area, which may
probably have been intended for use by a left-handed person.

References have been made earlier to the innumerable complete tools and
waste fragments, suggesting habitation sites and chipping-floors. Instances of
several hundred individual finds are fairly common. Even before the present
field work was undertaken, a collection of at least 10,000 flints, found locally,
had been brought into Clun Museum, with a further 3,000 collected by the
late Mr. Jonas Cooper from Clunbury parish. The vast numbers collected
surely indicate the suitability of the environment to the needs of the users,
and they must represent but a modicum of the original weight of nodules
obtained, and point to the volume of traffic and trade along the trackways in
these parts. The following unusual find may possibly have some bearing on
trading procedure in the Stone Age. It came to light some forty years ago
around Bucknell in Shropshire. A farmer was digging a hole for a field gatepost, and at the bottom he dug out two stones, both now in Clun Museum.
One of them is large and ovate, about 8-10 inches (20-25 cm) in diameter, and
2 inches thick (50 mm); it has five half-inch depressions on one convex face.
The other is about $2\frac{1}{2}$ inches (63 mm) in diameter, flat and thin, with five small
holes bored through it in the same pattern as the larger one. No supporting
evidence of soil context is available, but one could possibly conclude that when
travelling groups of men visited a settlement along the trackway, they bartered
some of their flint nodules for, say, a heap of skins. They could take with them

[2] A similar set of tools was recovered by the author at the Stanton-on-the-Wolds
site (*vide ibid.* Trans. Thoroton Soc.) 1972.

the small stone and leave the larger one on the heap until they returned after 'selling out' their flints further along the route. They would then hand in the small one in order to claim the skins which they had earlier bought. The stones could thus be interpreted as a kind of tally. Having holes bored through, the small tally could be threaded and tied to their person to avoid it being mislaid.

The depth of furrow in ploughing is all-important in searching for specimens. A few flints which have come to the surface in a localised area of a field generally indicate that the ploughshare had only just reached the upper limits of the 'floor', whereas a more dense concentration denotes penetration by the plough to the original base of the floor. Many floors may be located next to a modern field hedge, so that a watch should be kept on the possible continuation of the site into the next field, if it should ever be ploughed. Frequent visits at each stage of cultivation are rewarding. New flint specimens may be released from the compacted furrow, made even more easy to discern if rain had fallen just previously, washing them and making them more lustrous. It was found to be a great help to accustom the eye to detecting flakes if a few are carried and dropped onto the ground and studied assiduously for a few moments and picked up again before commencing a search. Then by marking the genuine find-spot of each with a peg and working round each peg in turn, the pattern of distribution could be obtained, and the site margins fixed.

Land prepared for root-crops gave the best results, as cultivation extended over longer periods, and the tilth was finer than for cereals; the crop was sown on ridges, giving a double soil surface exposure; hoeing against weeds frequently brought to view many more specimens; one could also walk up and down between ridges without damage to the crop after the seed had germinated; one's search was directed in narrow straight lines without risk of meandering and missing any lying on the surface. This could not be done in a field sown with cereals or *brassicae*, such as kale or rape, which soon cover the ground.

There remains the incidence of the stray finds whose distribution and recovery appears to be fortuitous. Apart from finding arrowheads *in situ*, they can be found anywhere. Possible explanations are that they are specimens lost by primitive hunters who missed their quarry, or that they were carried away in wounded animals. The presence of occasional single flakes or implements may be explained further by the probability of their being carried from their original site inside compacted clods of soil in the horses' feet or, in more recent times, in the rubber cleats of the tractor, or in soil adhering to the various implements used in preparing a seed-bed. They are more likely to have been carried downhill in this way and dropped free when turning on the 'headlands' of a field.

In searching for flint sites in the fields, the collector at times may find specimens of stone, rather than of flint. These artefacts are usually found singly, and they cannot with any certainty be attributed to any definite period. The most common is the spindle-whorl, made of sandstone usually, circular in shape, with a central hole of hour-glass pattern denoting that it was bored through by drilling from both faces, and with an overall diameter of around two inches (50 mm.). They are found mainly near to streams with a settlement not too far away; one, in fact, was found by the author's family thrown up in a mole-hill. They were probably used by the womenfolk when spinning wool.

Much larger than the spindle-whorl, but of similar form, circular and holed, is the mace-head. Their distribution is sporadic, and they were probably used for ceremonial purposes. Other holed stones of quite an appreciable weight, circular or nearly so, are at times encountered. These, however, are comparatively modern and were used to weight down the thatch on ricks or roofing. Thus, any stones which have holes bored through them are indeed worthy of recovery.

In the manufacture of hammer- or axe-heads flint was not always used—in fact, flint would fracture under a hammer blow. Axeheads, however, with a sharp cutting edge, were made of flint, and the secondary flaking resulting from their manufacture was, in the process of time and improved techniques, polished to a smooth finish. But suitable alternative rock was also commonly used, chiefly a hard fine-grained rock. In this area is situated the supply source of the Hyssington picrite rock from which so many axe-hammers, found all over Britain, have been manufactured. These have been scheduled as Type XII by Professor F. W. Shotton, formerly Head of the Geology Department at Birmingham University, a leading authority on prehistoric stone implements. It is a major disappointment that the actual site of the axe factory is not located. The matter was discussed with Mr. T. Smith, of Newcastle-on-Clun, who remembered as a boy 'seeing heaps of stones with holes in them' in about 1890, but he could not remember the spot nor describe it from maps; nor could he be persuaded to re-visit his boyhood home near to Brithdir on Stapley Hill. For the time being, therefore, all that is known is that the site has been seen within living memory, that it is near to Brithdir, and that it is now probably overgrown.

At this stage, reference should be made to another stray flint which the worker may find difficult to interpret at first sight. This is the later gun-flint, and deserves a place in the records. In the days of the flint-lock gun, prehistoric flint knife or scraper blades were picked up on the land, and, by snapping off the two ends, a portion from the centre about half to one inch square was obtained. This was ideal for fitting into the striking mechanism of such guns to create the spark which flashed the powder. Those that have been found were generally near to buildings or in gardens. It should be noted that, in snapping off the two ends of the prehistoric flint blade, modern man has lost the bulb of percussion, and one can only infer from the general appearance of the flake portion that it has been so converted. Its location site also has been lost, though it is likely to have been local.

Natural phenomena can also provide clues in field-work in a number of ways. Whilst these are many, a few examples will serve to illustrate the importance of being aware of their value. The soil excavated by a fox or by rabbits should at least be cursorily examined in passing. One never knows what may have been thrown out by the animal in penetrating a site. The mole-hill, too, is a clear example, but the mole, working in a grass field, would not be active on the line of under-lying lost roads, trackways and the like, due to consolidated soil conditions. Buried stonework associated with hill-forts, or the foundations of long lost buildings, or even of buried monoliths, will be impervious barriers to the mole. Molehill activities will stop short of such obstacles, and we can then look for a clear plan of such items beneath the turf. Once soil has been disturbed, it is tantamount to a form of cultivation. Plant life will, therefore, be encouraged and develop more vigorously, a feature which can often be seen on the ground, and even more so from the air photograph. Ground frost will thaw quicker from such ground than over anything cold beneath the surface.

## CHAPTER IV.

## THE RIDGEWAY

ACROSS the area from east to west is a section of a clearly defined prehistoric ridgeway, variously called the Springhill, Onibury to Anchor, or even the Clee Hill ridgeway. Its origin is clearly Neolithic, but it is really a kind of spinal cord for the area, from which the various phases of history radiate to form the pattern of man's activities for at least the past 5,000 years. References to the ridgeway have already been made and others will be made more fully later, so that at this juncture a detailed itinerary is now indicated for identification purposes.

It can be traced from Wiltshire, over the Clee Hills (Shropshire), and one can join it conveniently at Onibury (6 m. N. of Ludlow), and proceed westwards towards Brandhill, where any of the south-facing fields under the plough below Goat Hill on the 1,000 ft. contour can yield many flints. At the 'Crossways', the ridgeway passes over Watling Street in its south-bound course to Caerleon. Beyond Clungunford, its course is not clearly marked, but would appear to follow a footpath through Abcott Farm, then west of the railway in a straight line to a sharp bend on the present lane to Three Ashes. Here, in the triangle, where the ridgeway joins the B4385, are to be seen three ash trees planted close together (one being sadly decayed in 1953). Each grows in a different parish—Clungunford, Clunbury and Hopton Castle.

Westwards over B4385 and at the Grid ref. SO 364784, the field north of Hopton Castle and the adjoining two to the east once formed one of the Saxon common fields. By following the clearly defined lane past Llantop, the area around the Llan could still prove very rich in antiquities, in spite of the very many flints which have already come to light. Even twenty years ago, over 400 flints in Clun Museum had been recovered from nineteen fields in this area. They were mostly from Wiltshire, but some were of Irish origin, which seems to suggest 'trading' in both directions along the ridgeway. Their sites were concentrated around the pools and the well. The two monoliths north of the house are not prehistoric, but glacial erratics of Rhayader grits. Incidentally this area around the Llan serves as a good example of how the field worker may pick up clues to other finds apart from those of primary interest. In examining the Llan in relation to the ridgeway as the prime objective, the following secondary observation was made. About 1950, some very fine old yew trees were felled, and these, together with the earthworks in the second field to the north, suggest a Celtic church settlement long-since decayed, but providing a link in the occupational continuity from prehistoric to modern times.

Beyond Cwm Barn, along the southern flanks of Sowdley Wood, and then south-westwards to Fountain Head, a major nucleation of monoliths is encountered (as shown on the Clun nucleation map—Fig. 3).

From the many studies in the field, the author offers here a suggestion regarding the purpose of these megalithic *meini hirion*, by referring to their agricultural rôle and their siting near to the sources of minor streams—features well illustrated in this area by this example. Many of these large stones do not appear on the maps, and their recognition is the result of fieldwork and the application of this suggestion.

Westwards over the cross-roads, past Penywern Farm and over Clun Hill,

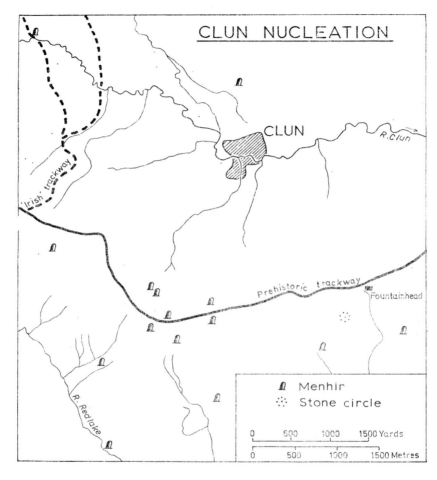

Figure 3

is the area where many of the first flints to be placed in Clun Museum were found by a former headmaster of Clun, George Luff, especially in the 'Camp Field'. At SO 297790, a huge monolith (14 ft. high, 4 ft. wide and 2 ft. thick) was buried in 1865, and its position can be seen as a cropmark in a dry season. On joining the A488 main road from Knighton to Clun, a small earthwork camp may be seen in the corner of the southern field. For a few yards, this short length of main road superimposes the ridgeway, until the latter resumes its independent course north-west along the eastern and northern flanks of Rockhill. Immediately before reaching the Burfield cross-roads, is found a recumbent menhir, known locally as the 'Heartstone', at SO 278796; it is 900 ft from the spring, and measures 8 × 7 × 2½ ft. It is one of the 'female' type, as Alexander Kieller describes such megaliths of similar shape at Avebury. This one may be associated with the traditional fertility of the area, where early agriculture is thought to have reached a high level of efficiency. From the stone radiated important local routes, e.g. N.E. via Weston to the Whitcott menhir near the river Clun at SO 276824 along a link trackway (seen best just before sunset) to the 'Irish' ridgeway to the north, or S.E. to the 'Camp Field' flint site and Penywern stone circle, or N.W. along the Springhill section of the main ridgeway, which we are following, to the Kerry Hills and its stone circles.

Beyond the signpost to Burfield farm, on the terraces in the second field on the north side of the road as far as the quarry, the author and family found an impressive concentration of some 200 flints. Judging from the variation in patination and size, they appear to indicate an extensive period of occupation in the Neolithic and Early Bronze Ages. In a mile, Springhill farm is reached, where the ridgeway passes at 1,300 ft. through a gap in Offa's Dyke, obviously intended as such in its construction.

Proceeding westwards along Spoad Hill, past the farm at Stonypound, the ridgeway swings round the 1,335 ft. contour past a roadside belt of conifers, with a superb view of the Clun Valley as far west as the Anchor. This section, above all others, serves to emphasise the ideal routing for a ridgeway. South of the Dowke Hill, only some 50 ft. below its summit, the route is virtually straight to the cross-roads at Betws-y-crwyn.

This is the centre of a very large parish, its size being determined in the following manner. At the Cantlin Stone (SO 203869) is a memorial stone, which has in modern times been erected within a few feet of the earlier one which marks the spot where in 1691 a pedlar was found robbed and dead. He was buried under a yew tree on the south side of the churchyard, because Mainstone parish refused to do so. Eventually, when the land here was in dispute at the time of the Enclosure Act of 1875, Betws-y-crwyn claimed the land because it had buried this pedlar in its churchyard many years before, on Mainstone's refusal. The pedlar was known only as 'William', and 'C' was added to signify that no one 'can tell' what his surname was. This was later expanded to 'Cantlin'.

Pausing at the cross-roads, one realises that, although there are quite a number of farm-houses and cottages around, very few can be seen, as they are hidden, especially in the Quabbs area which is a typical Celtic settlement. The church, below which at Ladywell is the holy well with healing properties, was originally thatched, as witnessed by the brackets on the north wall, on which rested the hooked pole by which the thatch could be torn off in the event of fire. Inside, the roodscreen, pews and pulpit are worthy of inspection. Its name means 'the chapel of the skins', reminiscent of the method of payment to itinerant monks from Abbey Cwmhir for services rendered in the form of skins or wool.

In a short distance, a lane forks south past Llanllwyd Farm, where, east of a former L-shaped spinney of old conifers adjoining the buildings, an area is enclosed by a dressed stone wall, continuing over the three adjoining fields to the north-west. Inside the spinney area are some depressions which compare very closely with those forming the Cattle Pound at $\frac{3}{4}$ mile W.N.W., to which this lane leads directly.

But, from the fork the ridgeway proper is the northerly road, reaching a height of 1,400 ft. for a mile to the next cross-roads. Here, in the field at the north angle was found in 1955 a large grey leaf-shaped arrowhead. In the same field at SO 185835 is the site of the 'Grey Stones' stone circle, described later in detail. In fact, the amount of material which has come to light as a result of field-work here emphasises beyond doubt the intense activities of prehistoric man along the margins of this ridgeway. At this point, one has only to digress along the Forestry track which skirts the southern margin of Betws Hill Wood to see the site where the author and family in 1954 discovered prehistoric habitations, notably at SO 175840 five inches below the surface revealed by the plough. At SO 168843 within a circular site, 20 yards in diameter, some 40 flints were retrieved six inches below the surface, and at SO 173841 219 were obtained from an 8 yard diameter circle at five inches deep.

As the ridgeway passes by the Anchor Inn, one can see the well in the back yard from which rises the infant river Clun at 1,250 ft. above sea level, before turning along the ridgeway which has superimposed upon it in this section a short length of the present main road as far as the English-Welsh boundary. Here one turns north past Rose Grove Wesleyan Chapel heading for Kerry Pole, in an area where there is a complex of tumuli and stone circles. Beyond, the ridgeway is preserved in the track of a right-forking footpath to Panty-llidiart, where it joins, and forms part of, the B4368 road, as it did earlier at the Anchor. Over twenty miles of this prehistoric highway across our study area has been followed. It began at 300 ft., and, having climbed to 1,400 ft. at one point, it has descended to 500 ft.

CHAPTER V

# THE ORIENTATION AND MATHEMATICS OF ANCIENT CULTS

IN recent years, it has become abundantly clear that prehistoric man has left behind evidence that his intelligence had, until very recently, been much under-rated. It is from the later phase of the Neolithic and the overlap into the earlier phase of the Bronze Age that our evidence is derived. At this time, a succession of immigrant agricultural peoples moved into Britain from western Europe, using the western sea-routes. Their culture was marked by an elaborate cult of the dead, using huge stones to form vaults; the culture was thus called Megalithic. The monuments of this culture, particularly in Wales, are heavily concentrated. Big stones were used, not only in the construction of burial chambers, but in the setting up of free-standing stone circles, stone alignments, and single standing stones (known also as *meini hirion*). The purpose of the first group is self-explanatory, but there has for long been an element of doubt as to the true purpose of the second group. Sir Norman Lockyer, an eminent antiquarian at the turn of the century, was convinced that the stone rows, stone circles and standing stones had at least some connection, by reason of their orientation, with both solar and lunar positions. As more thought was applied to such theories, it became progressively more logical to assume that the Megalithic agriculturalists would require such methods for seasonal computation. It was found that, irrespective of the type of inhumation megaliths in this area and beyond, the stone circle and the menhir were fairly general in distribution. They were frequently sited up the side-valleys of tributaries of the major rivers, on the better alluvial fringes bordering such streams, and within easy access to springs, as is shown in the Clun nucleation map (Fig. 3). It was in such environments that hitherto undetected monoliths were recognised.

Scholars have in recent years devoted much attention to the mathematics and geometric principles on which the siting of these free-standing megaliths appear to have been based, and, although not fully accepted by all, their theories are, nevertheless, gaining wider acceptance. A growing volume of literature is available, the details of which are beyond the scope of this work. Nevertheless, the field worker can make very good use of the geometric principles put forward by applying them, or at least bearing them in mind, when searching for traditional sites of long-forgotten or disappeared megalithic

*21*

monuments. It was in this way that the writer was able to locate the lost stone circle on the Kerry Hills, and to point to the possible site of yet another circle in the same complex. Elsewhere in Wales beyond this area, other possible sites are being revealed by using these geometric principles and relevant alignments.

Professor A. Thom, the pioneer of this study, formulated the basic structural unit used in the Megalithic Age as being 2.72 feet (0.829 m.), which he refers to as the megalithic yard. Quite frequently, a larger unit of 6 MY is used (16.3 feet), which is comparable to the English rod of 16.5 feet. The principles of the Pythagorean triangle seem to have been known to Megalithic peoples long before Pythagoras himself. Lyle B. Borst recognised that the earliest ground plans of certain cathedrals in Europe, especially those with an apse at the east end and on both transepts, were very similar to the plans of henge monuments, if the half-circle of the apse is extended to the full circle. He found that the centres of these three circles formed a Pythagorean triangle. Based on this, he suggests that such Christian sanctuaries actually rest upon earlier henge monuments. It is well-known from the many circular church-yards in Wales, for example, that Christianity adapted Pagan concepts in this way.

These patterns appeared so consistent in extant plans of both Megalithic and Christian sanctuaries that the writer conceived the idea that it might be possible in some circumstances to use a geometric approach to bring to light megalithic sites which are either totally unknown, virtually lost over the years, or known only vaguely from antiquarian tradition.

Such a problem had concerned the writer for some 25 years regarding the stone circles on the Kerry Hills of the Montgomery/Shropshire border (Nat. Grid SO 157861). The extant stone circle, consisting of a centre stone surrounded by a ring of eight others, was noted by Hancock some 100 years ago, and appears on the R.C.A.M. plan. At the same time, Hancock also records the remains of a second similar circle in line with the extant one and the tumulus known as 'Shenton's Tump'. One of the stones he concluded from his drawing was the central one and at the time he saw five others, two of which appeared to be out of position. This site, therefore, appeared ideally suited to the writer to develop the Thom/Borst ideas in reverse as it were. In fact, it could just be possible that the missing fragments of a uniform pattern of circles might be located by superimposing the standard pattern upon the terrain. Examination of the air photograph (Figure 4) revealed as a crop-mark the position of Hancock's missing circle (Figure 5) beyond doubt. Its similar pattern of dots corresponded, and furthermore, there were other dots indi-

Figure 4—Air photograph of Kerry Hills (Mont) concentration of stone circles and tumuli ; (A) existing circle; (B) Hancock's disappeared circle; (C) possible unknown circle; tumuli at Blackwood, Kerry Pole, Shenton's & cropmark of ploughed out one. Old London coachroad & Springhill ridgeway cross at Kerry Pole.

cating other stones which could well have gone below the turf in Hancock's day. Here was an opportunity to see what geometry could offer by way of further revelations and observations. The method used is now given stage by stage, with reference to the plan, as taken direct from the field notes.

A line from centre stone A to centre stone B measured 100 MY. By dividing equally at 50 MY, each half could be used to form the basis of a Pythagorean triangle of 5 ten-unit MYs. Borst had found that a 5/12/13 ratio was very frequently used; and so, from this point on the line AB at W, a line was drawn at right angles to a point C exactly 12 ten-units of MY. C was found to coincide exactly with a hitherto unnoticed dot on the air photograph around which was an arrangement of seven dots. Was this a third circle C, similar to A and B, unrecognised and unknown?

At this stage, all identifiable stones and probable positions as crop marks comprising the perimeters of each circle were allocated a numbered letter. Thus, the perimeter stones of each circle A, B and C bear the appropriate lower-case letters in addition to numbers—e.g. a6 is no. 6 stone in the perimeter of circle A. The following facts were then noted.

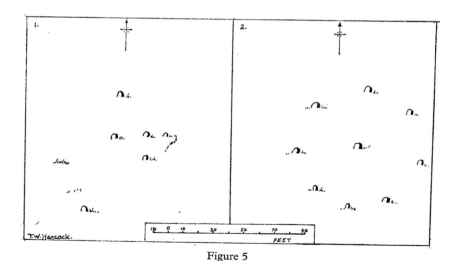

Figure 5

Two stone circles as seen and delineated by T. W. Hancock, (*vide* Montgomery Collections vol. XXIII 1889 pp. 82-84), on the Kerry Hills, Montgomeryshire.
No. 1.   now disappeared, but described by T.W.H.
No. 2.   still existing.

1.  Geometry :  Describe a circle from W with a radius AW.
    Result    :  This intersects AC at Z, BC at X and CW at V.
                 Z is the only point on AC from which a right angle
                 can be taken to B; and X is the only point on BC
                 from which a right angle can be taken to A. Lines AX
                 and BZ cross at Y which is itself on line WVC.

2.  Geometry :  Take V as centre with radius VA or VB and draw
                 circle.
    Result    :  This passes through stones a2 and b2, and also quite
                 near and equidistant to c3 and c6.

3.  Geometry :  Describe a circle based on X with radius AX.
    Result    :  This passes through c3 and c5.

4.  Geometry :  Describe a circle based on Z with radius BZ.
    Result    :  This passes through c4 and c6.
                 (At this stage, we have not only centre stone C, but
                 also 4 possible stones of that circle plotted by
                 geometry—c3, c4, c5 and c6.).

5.  Geometry :  Describe a circle from point V with radius to a4.
    Result    :  This passes not only through b4, but also through c2.

6.  Geometry :  Describe a circle from Z with radius Zc1.
    Result    :  This passes through b3 and b4.

7.  Geometry :  Describe a circle from X with radius Xc2.
    Result    :  This passes through a3 and a4.

8.  Geometry :  Describe a circle from V with radius Va6.
    Result    :  This passes through b7, and also through c4 and c5.

*Stone Alignments* :

| | | | | | |
|---|---|---|---|---|---|
| (i) | a7 and a5 | are aligned with centre | | | C. |
| (ii) | b6 and b8 | ,, | ,, | ,, ,, | C. |
| (iii) | b2 and b3 | ,, | ,, | ,, ,, | C. |
| (iv) | a2 and a3 | ,, | ,, | ,, ,, | c2. |
| (v) | b6 and b8 | ,, | ,, | ,, ,, | C. |

|        |             |    |    |    |    |      |
|--------|-------------|----|----|----|----|------|
| (vi)   | a3 and b6   | ,, | ,, | ,, | ,, | A.   |
| (vii)  | B and b8    | ,, | ,, | ,, | ,, | a5.  |
| (viii) | a6 and a4   | ,, | ,, | ,, | ,, | b7.  |
| (ix)   | c4 and c1   | ,, | ,, | ,, | ,, | b9.  |
| (x)    | c2 and c3   | ,, | ,, | ,, | ,, | b1   |
| (xi)   | c1 and c6   | ,, | ,, | ,, | ,, | a1.  |
| (xii)  | c5 and c7   | ,, | ,, | ,, | ,, | b8.  |
| (xiii) | b4 and b7   | ,, | ,, | ,, | ,, | A.   |
| (xiv)  | b5 and b6   | ,, | ,, | ,, | ,, | a4.  |
| (xv)   | b3, B & b8  | ,, | ,, | ,, | ,, | a5.  |
| (xvi)  | b1 and b9   | ,, | ,, | ,, | ,, | a1.  |
| (xvii) | a1 and a4   | ,, | ,, | ,, | ,, | c2.  |
| (xviii)| c1 and c6   | ,, | ,, | ,, | ,, | a3.  |
| (xix)  | c3 and Z    | ,, | ,, | ,, | ,, | a4.  |
| (xx)   | a4, b5 b6   | ,, | ,, | ,, | ,, | a6.  |

*Tumuli/Circle Alignments*:

(a) W to C to Block Wood.
(b) C to Shenton's to Kerry Pole.
(c) Block Wood to B to ploughed-out tumulus.
(d) Cefn Craig to Block Wood to C (via V, Y & W) to Rose Grove.
(e) Gwernesgob to C to ploughed-out tumulus.
(f) Two Tumps (at 1657 O.D.) to C to Shenton's.
(g) A to B to Shenton's.
(h) c1 to c3 to Shenton's.
(i) c4 to C to Shenton's.
(j) a5 to b4 to Shenton's.

(All above sites are on 1" O.S. sheet no. 128, or $2\frac{1}{2}$" sheet no. SO 18).

It may be worth noting as a possible clue to the original constructional planning that point V, forming two isosceles triangles, appears to be highly important. Not only does it appear in 4 of the 'geometry results' above, but also compass bearings from it point due east to the centre stone B and due south to the centre A. It is quite possible that there may prove to be a stone (or rock outcrop) at V from which the whole complex was computed. Hence Professor Thom's emphasis on the tracing and recording of every monolith should not be lightly ignored.

*Summary*

In view of the many geometric patterns, stone alignments and tumuli alignments, it would seem more than fortuitous that . . .

(a)  the existing circle A is an essential vital portion of a larger complex of circles;

(b)  the Hancock record of B was correctly interpreted as the remains of a circle (the two inner stones would seem to be displaced from the perimeter);

(c)  there is a circle at C either *in situ* below present ground level, or (even if removed to construct adjacent field boundary) the site is correct, being substantiated by crop-marks where each stone stood.

(d)  Regarding the details of circle B, it seems more than likely that b2, b3, b5, b7 and b9, showing as dots on the air photograph, do in fact mark the sites of stones (a) as cropmarks, if removed, or (b) still *in situ* but buried at Hancock's visit. All are involved in alignments and /or geometric patterns through major focal points. There may even be others not revealed.

(e)  Regarding the presupposed circle C, it should be emphasised that nothing is known of it in legend, tradition or record. The photograph does, however, suggest a pattern of dots so clearly conforming to circle A. It is sited exactly at the apex of the Pythagorean triangle with the ratio of 5, 12 and 13 so commonly used by megalithic sanctuary builders, the actual apical point resting upon the centre C. Each of the perimeter stones, c1 to c7 (and there may well be others not revealed), figures very prominently in alignments with others in the 3-circle complex, and also in alignments with the eight known tumuli in the area visible from the site, and possibly to two others revealed by the photograph, but awaiting detailed examination in the field. Again, not only is circle C involved in each of the above Nos. 1-8, but also appears in 12 out of 20 stone alignments, and in 7 out of 10 tumuli/circle alignments. Thus, it would appear that, in spite of being hitherto unknown, a circle at C is indeed highly probable and should be revealed on excavation.

(f)  In circle A, the perimeter stones a2 due east and a6 due west present the edge of each to the centre, whereas the others present a flat face. This phenomenon may logically be found to be repeated in circles B and C, if located by future investigators. Stone a1 at the south-east is a double one, face to face with about 5 inches clearance between the two. It does not appear to have been split.

(g)  The pattern of this complex so conforms to the symmetry of mega-lithic and Christian sanctuary plans that it commends itself to the professional archaeologist. Circle A and outlying tumuli are scheduled ancient monuments, and if these deductions are event-ually substantiated, it would prove that the Thom/Borst concepts are capable of contributing to a still wider field of research into lost knowledge in prehistoric and protohistoric matters by indicating features which might otherwise remain unsuspected. For example, one is more and more convinced that the recumbent megalith known as the 'Heartstone' at SO 278796, some $8\frac{1}{2}$ miles to ESE, is closely related to the Kerry Hill circles.

(h)  Preliminary investigations, subsequently conducted, have been concentrated on B and C, where probing appears to indicate the presence of sunken large stones.

In an attempt, so far, to locate unknown circle sites, this Kerry Hill complex appeared to present such strong possibilities of finding a third circle where two are known to exist, that the idea of repeating the technique elsewhere seemed provocative. Could such a study resolve various field problems of tradition or hear-say ? Could preliminary work on the drawing board circum-vent much laborious and abortive fieldwork, so necessary in these fast moving times of agricultural development and environmental upheaval ? Could one logically conclude that megalithic structures follow a definite geometric pattern into which one can predetermine the position, before undertaking detailed fieldwork, of a missing feature in the pattern ?

Should it eventually be decided that excavation of this area is justifiable professionally around the extant circle, then it might also be undertaken at other sites in Wales, notably at Ysbyty Cynfyn in Ceredigion, and around Bryn Celli ddu in Anglesey, which the author has provisionally investigated by the same techniques with comparable success. In the wider application of geometry, it seems highly logical to suggest that, throughout the Celtic Lands at least, a network of such patterns might well be established. What is possibly a micro-pattern locally might itself well prove part of a British macro-pattern embodying Stonehenge, Prescelly, Woodhenge, Arminghall and Callanish, and even beyond to a European one based on Carnac. At the moment, we are only just appreciating that Megalithic Man had a far deeper understanding of geometric patterns than was hitherto conceded. While this is a professionally scientific study, it in no way removes the chance of revealing unknown monuments, which is the prime objective of the field worker.

A few general observations may, at this stage, be given regarding the techniques of a more practical application in the field in finding the sites of lost megalithic monuments. Complaints by farmers that their ploughshares had struck a sizable stone under the soil have generally been fruitful, as in the field known as the 'Oaks', near Clun. They are very often recumbent monoliths. Many standing stones were frowned upon by agriculturalists in the last century as being obstacles to cultivation. Some were shattered by explosives, and their more manageable fragments removed to the field boundaries,—a place to look where a traditionally known stone is now missing. A few larger ones, which escaped this treatment for some reason or another, such as being superstitious when a thunderstorm intervened, were dropped by digging round their bases and toppled over prostrate into a prepared trench, and thus buried *in situ*. Their resting places can be seen in a dry summer when the crop (turf or cereal), growing upon it in the superficially thin soil overlay, burns off by dehydration, leaving a light brown patch within the surrounding green.

A roughly circular grass-covered area of a few yards in diameter on a hillside, which may be otherwise covered in bracken (*Pteridium aquilinum*) or heather (*Calluna vulgaris*) is always worthy of closer inspection with the aid of a soil-augur, or a bayonet, which is even better, as a probe. The patch of free grass denotes that the under-lying soil has at some time past been disturbed from a more compact virgin state.

Care must be taken in deciding whether some of the larger stones were glacial erratics, rather than megaliths surviving from megalithic times. Examination shows that the latter have unweathered butts, originally in the ground, (Fig. 6) with the part above the ground highly weather-worn, especially on the edge facing the westerly prevailing winds. A genuine recumbent monolith could, therefore, be re-erected in its original upright position. Having assessed its genuineness, one should attempt to explain its location for one's own satisfaction. Is it orientated in such a way that from it can be seen other monuments ? An outstanding record in this inventory is the 'Heartstone' (456), so named from its shape, a huge recumbent specimen on Rockhill near to the Springhill ridgeway, which illustrates extremely well the orientation factor and its use as a primitive signpost, irrespective of any other purpose which might be revealed by excavation. It may have been intended to point to the Whitcott Keysett stone (Fig. 7), which itself may or may not intentionally have marked the fording-place over the river Clun, as well as being orientated towards objects on the ridgeway and other landmarks.

Figure 6

Two Welsh examples of the 'male' type of menhir.


CHAPTER VI

BURIAL MOUNDS

IN the previous chapter it was noted that the Megalithic stone circle was built
up of large stones forming the perimeter of a circle, but were themselves free-

standing orthostats. It is possible that a 'stone circle' is so recorded on the O.S. maps, but, upon examination, the stones are, in fact, contiguous. These are generally the remains of the retaining kerb of a burial cairn. One such site was revealed by the writer in January 1945 by probing the supposed area, which had been depicted on the O.S. map as 'site of Grey Stones stone circle'. (379). On the ground was a circular area of grass surrounded by bracken. Such was the site as seen on that occasion, and it was not until the writer reported that it had been ploughed that it was in August 1955 proved by partial excavation to be a burial cairn with a circular composite stone-kerbed wall, as the accompanying plan reveals (Fig. 8). No actual burial cist was found, and, if one had survived the passage of time and the activities of grave-goods robbers, it is likely to be located off-centre to the circle around it. The cairn had been constructed with its kerb-walling prior to the formation of the hill-peat in the Bronze Age, when drier climatic conditions prevailed and the higher land was very congenial. The monument may possibly be comparable to the Pond Cairn in Glamorgan, and would then appear to be the most northerly example of this type. It does not appear on any maps earlier than 1833, when the O.S. map of the Clun district shows it as a ring of minute dots

Figure 7

The Whitcott Keysett menhir; an example of female dolmen idol in fertile valley, facing exactly due north before being pushed over in March 1944. (Nat. Grid. ref. SO 276824).

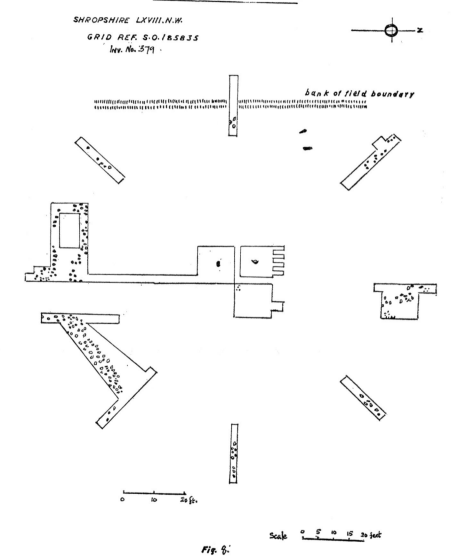

'GREY STONES' STONE CIRCLE.

SHROPSHIRE LXVIII.N.W.

GRID REF. S.O. 185835
INV. No. 379 ·

bank of field boundary

Fig. 8.

Excavation plan of 'Grey Stones' Circle.

under the name 'Grey Stones', and it is not printed in Old English type, as then used for antiquities. It was, however, seen prior to its destruction. Dr. O. G. S. Crawford, Archaeology Officer to the Ordnance Survey, writing in 1932 and quoting a report of 1884, states that 'only a few loose stones remain. The others have been removed'.

By giving the details of this particular site at some length, one can illustrate how the field worker rescued an ancient monument from what could easily have proved to be total oblivion. Had there been some action taken when reported in 1945, when the site was least disturbed, one might have obtained still more information than was found ten years later, after the plough had impinged upon it and dislodged the stones on the top of the kerb-walling. The 'dig' did, however, prove that the writer's opinion, expressed in 1945, was correct as to the site being nearer to the bank of the field boundary than the 1833 O.S. ring of minute dots indicated.

Round burial mounds of earth or stones, variously known as tumuli, cairns or barrows, are the most frequent occurrences of this Period, but one was constantly confronted with problems. Some were already shown on the maps, and it was only necessary to add supplementary information not so recorded or published. At times the map would show an antiquity as a tumulus, and in some of these instances the mound appeared much too high and flat-topped for a burial site. Pending future excavation, one could only, of course, merely suggest that it was likely to be an early mediaeval motte or castle mound, originally with a timber construction on it and surrounded by a stockade. (Examples of these are at SO 274999, 252954 and 334910.) Careful sighting might also disclose the former presence of a defensive ditch or moat around an outer bailey, long since weathered and almost filled. Such could belong to any period from the Bronze Age to the Iron Age, or even into Roman and Anglo-Saxon times. Along with an attempt at correcting description, it was noted at the time whether there were any signs of pilfering, which was an accepted practice in the case of barrows, even from Roman and Viking times up to the early 19th century.

Being a highly specialised undertaking, the excavation of a barrow can alone determine the period of dating and its contemporary ritual. Thus, all that the field recorder can do is to leave the site severely alone, and simply to report on the outward appearance of each; they fall into three classes:— bowl, bermed or saucer barrows. The first appears as an inverted bowl, often with a surrounding ditch, between which and the base of the mound is *no* intervening space. There are three types of bermed barrow :—bell, disc and bell-disc. While there is little visible difference usually, having regard to present-day degradation by weathering and interference, there is an important difference between the bowl and the bermed classes, in that in the case of the latter there is an intervening space from the base of the mound to the ditch. This is known as the berm. Also the disc and bell-disc types have a slight outer bank to the ditch, which is not found in the bell barrow. The third class,

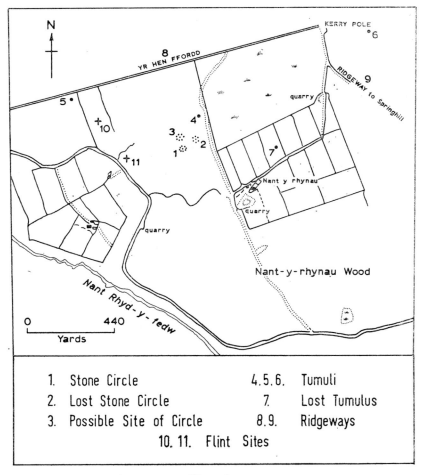

Figure 9

Sketch map of barrows (tumuli) in relation to other antiquities on the Kerry Hills.

the saucer or pond barrow, is found mainly in chalk areas, and is very flat. There is a tendency for tumuli to be found in groups near to 'henge sites, notably in the area under review around the Kerry Hill stone circles (Fig. 9).

We have discussed the incidence of the various profiles of burial sites, the authentic tumulus or cairn, and have drawn attention to those mounds which have been mapped as tumuli, but are, in fact, the mottes of early castles or forts. But there is still another form of mound of which the field worker should be aware. These are known as clearance cairns. They are generally encountered on high ground, and have the appearance of cairns—circular and turf-covered. They vary in diameter, and may range from a few in number to large groups. On probing, they are found to be formed with a stone core. The stones were, in fact, gathered from the land originally by early man, so that the land around the heaps could be cultivated by mattock-type implements in small plots by hand, in order to grow cereals. Needless to say, in the interests of verification, they should be recorded in preparation for excavation. It is probable that nothing will be found except a pile of stones, but a pollen-grain analysis of the soil beneath them may reveal the botanical species which were flourishing when the clearance took place, and from this analysis the presence of agricultural weed pollen will establish the fact that a form of cultivation was being undertaken at that time by very primitive methods in the intervening spaces. It is believed that such an extensive group of clearance cairns exists over the Hafod Ithel area at 1,100 ft. on Mynydd Bach in Ceredigion, which is beyond this special study area, but, nevertheless, typical of other sites in Britain as a whole, especially in Cumbria, the Pennines, North Yorkshire Moors and very generally in Scotland. A close watch should be kept by recorders with this background in mind.

Further problems occurred in that, near the main ridgeway, a series of mounds was known from old inhabitants to be spoil heaps from which tiles were quarried for roofing local buildings within living memory. Other mounds, too, proved to be drumlins or eroded portions of river terraces, or possible moraines (Inv. no. 401) as on the bank of the river Clun, shown as 'camp' on the O.S. maps.

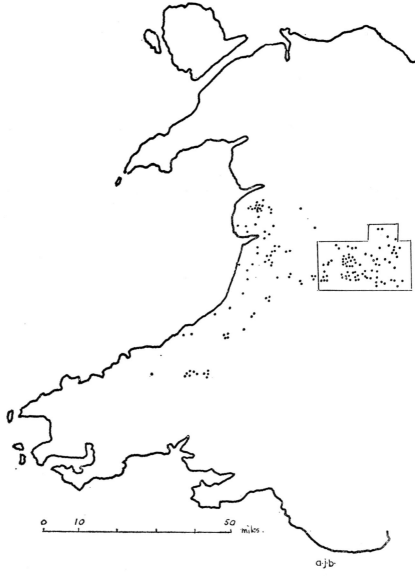

Figure 10
Sketch map of unrecorded burial sites.

The potential scope for discovering unrecorded tumuli and cairns, or for amending or supplementing information on them, is amply illustrated in the sketch map of the area (Fig. 10). Many are not obvious, being often over-grown with brambles or bracken or waste-land scrub in general. Careful sighting is advisable, and air photographs can be rewarding and informative.

The more the locations of many of the burial sites are examined, the more is one convinced that prehistoric man chose his burial sites with much thought. It was not by any means simply a 'vacant' piece of ground that he selected, many are found on the highest local ground where they can be seen on the skyline from several miles away, even though shrunken in size after millennia of weathering. Even the shallower types, such as the disc barrows would in their contemporary environment be visible at appreciable distances. If it were at all financially possible in the future to excavate each burial and to fix a constructional date and culture to each, much information would emerge as to the choice of such sitings. Again, the importance of alignments in selecting burial sites should not be overlooked. It is remarkable how many cairns so far examined are aligned with one another, or with definite stones within a stone circle. For example, by standing at the centre stone of a circle and sighting over another in its perimeter, one or more burial places may be seen in direct line. From the fieldwork undertaken, the inference is that successive occupants of an area, irrespective of their cultural practices, aligned their burials premeditatively with points in an existing stone circle, as found by the author on the Kerry Hills in Montgomeryshire[3] in particular, apart from other instances throughout the Principality. In fact, the rôle of the stone circle seems to be emerging as the Megalithic computer which provided unlimited information on the calendar, the seasons, astronomy and topographical directions.

## CHAPTER VII

## ROMAN AND NATIVE ACTIVITY

THE scarcity of finds of iron objects attributable to the various phases of the Iron Age is mainly due to the high degree of soil acidity. In general, the natural soil in western Britain, where not improved by modern techniques, is, on average, deficient by as much as two tons of calcium oxide $(CaO)$ per acre.

---

[3] *vide* Bird, A. J., 'Geometric principles and patterns associated with two megalithic circles in Wales'. *Britain in Patterns,* London, 1970.

The resulting corrosion has either completely destroyed iron objects or rendered them unrecognisable. A spear-head recorded at SO 245848, near to Gaer Din Ring camp at Newcastle-on-Clun, was submitted to W. F. Grimes (then Keeper of the London Museum) for examination and treatment. Whilst confirming it to be a spear-head, he passed it to J. W. Brailsford who could only hazard a possible date between the Early Iron Age and the Roman Period. It was a chance find and not correlated stratigraphically. Penetration of Iron Age culture, whether by the western maritime approaches or from the Severn Estuary northwards through the present Welsh-English border, was rather slow, and there was a relatively short interim period before the Roman subjugation, while bronze, as well as iron objects, remained in use.

Information and excavation reports on extant Iron Age sites can be consulted in many professional publications, and so, within the scope of this work, there is little to add except to report on conditions found at the time of the visit or on any incidental finds and observations.

A small, but useful sign to note in examining hill-forts is the presence of a single elderberry bush (*Sambucus niger*) growing within the ramparts, which may pin-point the former water spring from which the occupants of the fort obtained water. The spring may have long since silted up, leaving the ground just moist enough for a suitable habitat for the elder. On the other hand, a number of such bushes outside the camp would rather suggest the presence of a badger colony, and that the profusion of elders was encouraged by hyperacidity in the soil due to urination and excreta by the badgers, which go some distance from their setts in their innate habits of hygiene.

Within this area there is by tradition the enigmatical site of the last stand of Caratacus against the Romans under Ostorius. In reporting this military operation, the Roman historian Tacitus (*vide* Annalium Liber XII, chapters 34-35) mentions no actual place by name. It may, therefore, be appropriate to include here a brief summary of local legends, to be added to the many other interpretations put forward in an attempt to fix the site—*tot homines, tot sententiae* !

Briefly, the weight of local opinion tends to substantiate the views of Lt. Col. Burne, which he expressed from local tactical considerations. The suggestion is that Caratacus was based on the great hill-fort of Caer Caradoc above Chapel Lawn (midway between Clun and Knighton). While there, Caratacus received news that the Romans were moving south against him. He decided to hasten north, hoping to reach the second Caer Caradoc hill-fort at Church Stretton, and to intercept them there. Unfortunately for him, he was too late, and had to fall back and establish yet another defensive position rather hastily. His choice fell upon a section of rising ground south of the river Clun at Purslow, with Clunbury Hill on his eastern flank and the ridge of Purslow Woods to the west. His communications were good, because the Springhill main ridgeway was but a few yards behind him. The Romans advanced from the direction of Kempton as far as the river Clun. This is thought to have been in spate when they arrived. Even today with better drainage, this river rises very fast and is very highly coloured after heavy rain. From its source at the Anchor to Purslow, it falls from 1,260 to 550 feet (384 to 168 m.) in 12 miles (19.3 km.). It is, therefore, most likely to have presented a major obstacle in trying to find the fording place across, which Tacitus, with his usual terse phraseology, records as '*praefluebat amnis vado incerto*'. But, as is usual, the floods fall just as rapidly. The Romans (again quoting Tacitus) crossed it without difficulty—'*amnemque haud difficulter evadit*', and so engaged Caratacus on the heights ('*imminenta iuga*') south of the river. Their discipline and superior arms prevailed, and the suggested line of Caratacus' retreat can be followed through a sequence of place-names to the south. As the General Inventory forming the basis of this work is concerned solely with unrecorded material on the maps, the arguments for or against this theory of the 'last stand' are only relevant in so far as likely tracks or topographical details can be recorded in support.

The major Roman roads, based on the O.S. map of Roman Britain (1:625,000), have been shown (Fig. 11) for Central Wales from the coast to the English Border, in order to give clarity and an expansive context to the special area under review. Included, too, on this overall map are some fifty sites of unrecorded observations with possible Roman/ Native inter-relation associations, from which it is clear that for such a wide area there is only a very broad scatter, in spite of closer scrutiny in the special area. The records relating to former Roman finds include 37 coin recoveries, a hoard of 200, one Nerva coin, three querns, pottery and a bronze figurine of the period. Though not impressive, they do, however, point to areas of native trading and other contacts with the Romans away from the major road systems, which may assist future research in determining secondary route features. We know of the locations of Roman lead-mining operations, such as at Shelve in Shropshire, or on Cefn Pawl in Radnorshire. They must, therefore, have used or constructed extraction routes for metal mining. The search for clues for Roman subsidiary roads should thus constantly be kept to the fore by the field worker. Needless to say, opinions so expressed should have some factual support, such as place and field names, or finds. Local residents tend to define everything very old as being 'Roman', and too much reliance should not be placed on such statements in themselves, as other investigators have in the past jumped to erroneous conclusions, even to the point of constructing county maps of Roman road systems, based on the assumption that straight roads must be Roman in origin, though most are in fact modern.

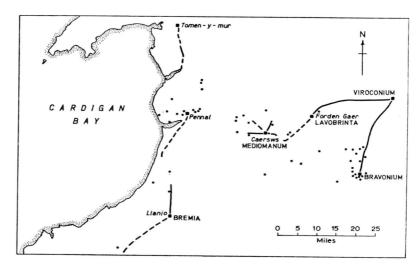

## NOTES ON THE MAP OF ROMAN RECORDS (Fig. 11)

There are three major Roman roads associated with Central Wales from the coast to the Borders,

    (a)   a portion of Watling Street in its southwards deflection from Viroconium, passing through this study area from Church Stretton to Bravonium.

    (b)   another from Viroconium westwards to Caersws and the Dyfi Estuary, again crossing the area.

    (c)   a third, outside the study area, but mentioned as a possible objective for the area roads, is Sarn Elen. This runs southwards from Tomen-y-mur to Bremia.

The sketch map shows the certain course sections, being shown as single continuous lines, while those in single pecked lines represent uncertain sections. To quote from the O.S. General Introduction to the map of Roman Britain "it is obvious that the road system of Wales requires more careful study to complete the line from Carmarthen to Caernarvon parallel with Cardigan Bay, and to show how this road was provided with the necessary strategic connections eastwards to the Severn Valley and the West Midlands". Preliminary work has been undertaken in 1976–1977.

The position of the 54 sites shown on the map indicates a concentration of general records in relation to the known sections of these three roads, while outliers would seem to point to roads subsidiary to them.

For details of the Roman stations in the broad Central Wales area, e.g. Tomen-y-mur, Pennal, Llanio, Forden Gaer and Caersws, *vide* Nash-Williams, V.E., *The Roman Frontier in Wales*, Cardiff, Univ. Wales Press, 1954 and subsequent revised editions.

While the Roman military and political administration ended in Wales in 383 A.D., many of Roman birth stayed on as settlers and blended into the community by inter-marriage. Their occupation was mainly agricultural, and from time to time evidence of the existence of a villa comes to light, which is likely to be succeeded by finds of other masonry or domestic fragments. In fact, native life went on much as before, especially in Wales. The portable finds are said to be either Roman or Romano-British, as in the example at Stowe, near Knighton on the Shropshire side of the river Teme.

As regards buildings, these can be detected by the study of air photographs, shown up in outline as a crop-mark over a parched area, but, on the ground, where the land has been under the plough, the scatter of rubbish, such as stones, plaster, broken tiles or pottery, may give the first tell-tale indication, apart from obstruction to farm implements in their soil penetration. Where the land is under grass, moles or rabbits may bring evidence to the surface, or even the pattern of nettle growth may give an indication. But detection, of course, depends on the depth of the overlying soil. The laying of drains or pipes in deep trenching should, therefore, be watched, while tactful enquiries from the people doing such work are often extremely rewarding. Villas are not the only potential finds, but also, in an organised Roman rural community, there could be farm buildings, and kilns for making tiles and bricks. A general observation is that the Romans, like the later builders of the abbeys and the monasteries, had a discerning eye for desirable building sites. Furthermore, it should be noted that, in an occupation period of around 400 years, Roman buildings could have been modified to suit alternative needs, as also were road routings over rivers and streams, depending on the type of traffic at different periods. A modern road does not necessarily overlie a Roman predecessor. In fact, it more usually runs alongside, which seems to suggest that in Anglo-Saxon times, the Roman roads, derelict or choked by vegetation, were left as direction indicators. The alignment of present field boundaries in open farm-land, or of early administrative boundaries, as on the Enclosure or Tithe Maps, may again suggest a connecting link between one or two known points on a former Roman road, and it would seem safe to assume that there must have been minor roads from known Roman buildings, as links with major roads of the period, and many such suggestions have been made in this record of the fieldwork undertaken.

## Chapter VIII

# THE BOUNDARY LINE OF CYMRU

THE period which follows the withdrawal of the Romans from Wales in 383 A.D., usually termed the Dark Ages, covers some 650 years, from the time when the Anglo-Saxons infiltrated into a land where the Roman administrative authority had ceased to operate, to the coming of the Normans. The foundation of the England that we know today was at that time being laid down and the Celtic Highland Zone was ruled by upstart Romano-British princes. The paucity of information is indeed reflected in the term Dark Ages, and here there is an open field in which to glean a harvest of information. From north to south in our area runs the great linear or travelling earthwork of Offa's Dyke (Clawdd Offa), which constitutes the line of definition between England and Wales determined at that time,—a major frontier over 100 miles (over 160 km.) from the Dee to the Bristol Channel, between the Welsh and the kingdom of Mercia under Offa, based on Tamworth. To this is related Wat's Dyke in the north, and also a number of lesser forward earthworks, (such as 'The Cross Dykes', 'Wantyn Dyke', 'Lower Short Dyke' and 'Upper Short Dyke'), on its west side, which give the impression of being thrown up athwart weak places of ingress from Wales, pending the completed construction of the Dyke itself. The whole complex has been comprehensively studied by Sir Cyril Fox, and, therefore, needs no further discussion, except to note in passing the smaller supplementary information, such as human or natural interference, gaps in the Dyke, and spoil-holes still visible. These observations have not only brought the records up-to-date archaeologically, but have enabled a watchful eye to be kept on damage, though this today is less likely to remain unnoticed for long, as the Dyke is now designated as a National Walking Route.

One small find of this period, worthy of mention, was obtained by my wife from the dried-up mud on the edge of a pond at Lane House, Mardu, near Clun in Shropshire, within sight of the Dyke. This is a Whitby jet bead, identified by Professor Christopher Hawkes as belonging to the VIIIth century A.D., and probably lost from a necklace worn by someone at the time of the Dyke's construction. The association with Whitby in Yorkshire and the Dyke of Central Wales is interesting and evocative, as so much of the

Welsh Borderland and Wales in general had cultural contacts with Northern England and South Scotland from Roman times onwards.

One of the highest priorities to which attention was devoted in the field was the recording of field-names from every possible source. This was essential, not only because of the risk of their being lost to knowledge, due to agricultural development, demanding the amalgamation of several fields into one large economical unit, but also because field-names often contain an implied reference to the existence of some antiquity or the location of a historical event. Closely allied to field-names were place-names, one of which is of particular interest to the Boundary Line of Cymru. This is Treverward, in a farming area in South Shropshire, between Clun and Knighton, on an old coachroad, and adjoining the deserted village of Burfield, destroyed by Owain Glyn Dŵr in 1401. The name Treverward was initially on record as a Saxon settlement known as Burwardston, and its subsequent change to Tref Burward indicates that the Welsh here took over from the Saxons. Another example of interest is on Shadwell Farm, where a portion of the Old Shadwell Township ends at the Dyke. The Weal in Weal's Old House (if not a direct Border surname) is probably derived from 'Weala', the Anglo-Saxon word for 'foreigner', and its location in the upper Clun valley is interesting as a possible reference to the Welsh raiders or settlers, from the English point of view. At Whitcott Keysett, near Clun, is a field known as Bryn Wicket, itself corrupted from Whitcott, containing a mound. This appears to be the *caput* of a Celtic habitation site of the pre-Norman '*ceisydd*'. If this is so, it would explain the village name as being the 'white dwelling of the *ceisydd*', who was the bailiff who collected the dues. The adjoining district hamlet of Mardu (=maer dy) is the house of the local mayor. Llanedric, a local farm nearby, contains the Welsh word 'llan', with its original meaning of 'enclosed land', before it evolved into the specific meaning of church land enclosures and thence to the church itself.[4]

This place, as it contains no known church site, would seem to refer to lands held by 'Wild' Edric, a Saxon thane. Gunridge, near Clunton, is probably a derivation from Gunward, the Saxon landowner *tempore regis Edwardi* in the Domesday Record under Clungunford. This area formed part of Gunward's Clun estates held under Picot de Say, from whom, incidentally, Hopesay and Stokesay get their names.

---

[4] For those interested in the association of Celtic words with those found in the Middle East, the word 'llan' is very significant in that the Arabic word for an enclosed compound adjoining a religious centre is 'khan', very similar to the pronunciation of 'llan' by people in North Wales. Furthermore, 'khan' itself is an earlier Persian word of similar meaning. Three examples of places are Baghdad, Karbala and Najaf where Harun al Rashid founded a shrine in the 8th C. at the tomb site of Mohammed's son-in-law.

While Offa's Dyke was the established boundary between Cymru and Mercia, we have so far, indicated only the general way in which the field recorder should look at place-names for clues as to past history, and have, in so doing, used random examples from the pre- and post-Offan periods. To revert, therefore, to the more specific examination of the probable contemporary picture which existed about the time of the Dyke's completion, one should look at the villages whose names are Saxon, and so develop a clearer picture of the Saxon-Celtic impact and blending as seen by place-name survivals. Ignoring settlements smaller than village status, and taking the county of Salop, as being the westernmost area of Mercia, bearing the brunt of confrontation problems with the Celts, place-names with Saxon, Old English or even Norse and Welsh forms in the county can be grouped as follows:

(a) Excluding Celtic names for natural features, such as cefn, uchaf, cwm, maen, moel, or llyn, there are about 32 in all, situated all in the western quarter of the county down the border, 9 of which are south of the Severn.

(b) Place-names ending in 'ton' (enclosure), or containing 'stoke' (stockade), 'bury' (fort), or both, comprise
   i.  35 ending in 'ton' south of, and 29 north of the Severn, all absent from the Welsh Border.
   ii. 2 north of and 1 south of the Severn containing 'stoke'.
   iii. 2 north of and 15 south of the Severn containing 'bury'.
   iv. 1 containing both 'stoke' and 'bury' south of the river.

(c) Those ending in 'ley' are 9 north of and 11 south of the river, along its banks in the wooded areas.

(d) 1 each in the north and south end in 'field'.

(e) 3 in the north and 4 in the south end in 'wood'.

(f) 7 contain 'hope' and are all in the southern uplands of the county.

(g) those containing 'hill', 'ness' or 'hales' total 9, of which 7 are in the northern plain.

(h) those ending in 'wardine' are only 4, all found in the northern plain, with one on the south border with Herefordshire.

Saxon settlements were known as 'hams' (homes), yet in Shropshire there are but four. Why more places did not have this name ending would appear at first inexplicable. But when it is realised that it behove them to seek their safety by fortification, and that they used alternative place-names to conceal their presence, the reason becomes more apparent. Thus, of the four 'hams', three were near to fortified posts. One can with confidence assume that the existence of such villages, summarised above, was to all intents and purposes a Saxon settlement pattern contemporary with the Dyke, and, furthermore, the analysis shows that the Saxon settlements were widely and fairly evenly spread over this 'buffer county' outpost of Mercia about the time of the Dyke's construction. It also shows that there was some degree of tolerance towards Celtic settlements being established possibly later east of the Dyke, set up as an agreed demarcation line, but nevertheless patrolled. It was to make things easier for the Saxon sentries that, whenever the Dyke is carried on a hillside, the slope is always *from* the Mercian border *towards* the Welsh territory, enabling the sentry to overlook the valleys below.

Although during the Dark Ages communities had settled into nucleations of varying sizes, even reaching town size in parts of Britain, simple villages are alone found in this area. The reasons which caused their failure to survive or expand are several. In the 11th century, the creation of the Royal Forests was the chief contributory factor; in the 12th century, the Cistercians founded their monasteries mainly in Upland Britain, and, as the well-documented acts of the Cistercian Order intimate, neighbouring villages were uprooted and re-established elsewhere. Favourable weather in the 13th century encouraged the expansion of arable cultivation, while the 14th century saw a reversal of this as harvests failed in wetter conditions. A little later came the Black Death, wiping out at least a quarter of the population. Then, in the 15th century came the local devastations along the Welsh Marches connected with the war against Owain Glyn Dŵr, while the enclosures for sheep farming in the 16th century also hurried the process of depopulation. Little wonder, therefore, that with at least 2,000 villages deserted over England and Wales quite a number have been, or are still to be identified within the area of this boundary with Wales—a major exercise in itself for the field worker.

The Domesday Inventory of 1086 A.D. came just in time to record the details of many villages before they disappeared by being over-run by the above catastrophes. Usually, no documentary help is available. In the field, one clue to a site may be a rough piece of land surrounded by arable ground. The timber, wattle and daub, used in the construction of buildings, have long since decayed, and the stonework above ground has been pillaged for use elsewhere. The contemporary economic situation precluded the laborious removal of foundations, which were in consequence left for rough grazing or were overgrown with scrub vegetation. The ramification of local tracks or primitive roads may focus on a central point, seemingly without purpose. The survival of a parochial name on the map may occur where no village today exists, or a surviving farm may preserve the basic spelling of the place.

In the path of modern earth-moving machinery, however, urgency in locating the maximum number of such lost settlements is today more imperative than ever. In this study area, four sites were detected from documents and field examination, while place names also assisted, as well as legendary folk memory. In an approximate square area, from Bishop's Castle in the north to Knighton in the south, and from Leintwardine in the east to three miles west of Clun in the west, evidence seemed so strong in four other cases that they are plotted on the accompanying map with notes (Fig. 12).

As Offa's Dyke is a main feature of the area, a brief description of it at this point should perhaps be made, with allusions to some of the observations noted to either side. For six miles southwards from Springhill on the ridgeway already described, and in the direction of Knighton in Radnorshire, the Dyke crosses Llanfair Hill where it reaches its highest point (1408 ft.) over its entire length from Clwyd to Gwent. Northwards, descending to the Clun Valley past Lower Spoad Farm, its crest is 24 feet high, but, as it enters the river plain, it peters out, either because of river erosion or intentionally using the flood plain as a natural boundary. Past Bryndraenog Farm it is well-preserved with its spoil-holes on the eastern side still noticeable. The stream rising north of Mount Farm at SO261843 has badly eroded the Dyke and certainly was deflected in its course when the Dyke was erected. At SO 247862 it is broken to allow the prehistoric 'Irish' trackway to pass through an original gap in its construction, the latter being the track round the northern flank of the Hergan, south-east to Three Gates Farm, and south by Swinbatch Farm and the ridge of the Cefns (*sic*) to the river Clun ford, Weston Farm and the Springhill ridgeway. At the Hergan, a curious 'patching-up' by the diggers of the Dyke appears to have taken place. It would seem that they erred in their alignment by some fifty yards, when joining up from the north and from the south. A weak bank, set at an odd angle, joins the work, which Sir Cyril Fox deduced to have been built by two separate gangs of diggers.

Northwards, it passes Mainstone church, where is kept the stone formerly used in a challenging trial of strength by the village youths. The 'main' part of the place-name is thought to be from the Welsh word 'maen' (stone), rather than from the Latin '*manus*' (hand). A mile beyond Edenhope Hill, two gaps are seen in the Dyke, the first to allow the lane from Edenhope to pass through, and the other is eleven yards wide presumably for valley drainage. On the 1,250 ft. contour, the London to Aberystwyth coachroad is reached, forming the old county boundary of Montgomery.

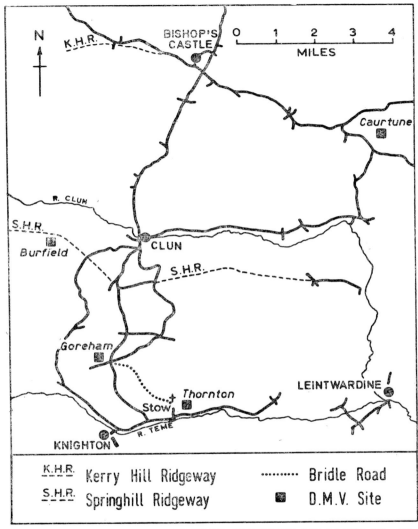

NOTES ON A GROUP OF FOUR DESERTED VILLAGES (Fig. 12)

Within the area shown on the map, fieldwork has brought to light the probable sites of four deserted villages, as follows :

A. GOREHAM (SO 283754).
This is believed to mark the site of the church and burial ground, to the east of which is an old milestone. The boundary brook is known as *Gore*

Gutter. In Eyton's '*Antiquities*' it is mentioned that in the Inquisition of 1272 or 1291 there is a township of 'Llangornes' in this district, but so far unidentified. *Garn* Cottages, just over ½ mile N.E., may also provide a clue. Within living memory the church site was referred to as 'Old Stow Church', and it is connected by an ancient bridle path to the present Stow Church.

B.   THORNTON (SO 22734).
This area is the most likely to establish the position of *Thornton* in the Domesday Survey, just E. of *Tornett* Wood, where the name is significant.

C.   CAURTUNE (SO 402853).
This lost manor of *Caur*tune of the Domesday Survey is probably around Upper *Car*wood farm. This place in 1393 is associated with the name of nearby Edgton, which was called 'Eggedun-juxta-*Caur*wood'.

D.   BURFIELD (SO 260802).
The position of the church profile and surrounding mounds indicates clearly the site of the village which was destroyed by Owain Glyn Dŵr in 1401. The present Burfield Farm represents the former Warren House, from which the Warren was supervised.

CHAPTER IX

# CASTLES OF EARTH AND STONE : ABBEYS AND CHURCHES : THE LEGACY OF THE NORMANS

THE castles, churches and monasteries associated with the Norman Age are very widespread, and their remains are usually visible above ground. For this period, naturally, there is an extremely wide range of publications on virtually every monument containing Norman features, e.g. the Ministry of Works for castles and monasteries, down to the historical guides which are to be found in most churches. But, in spite of this wealth of data, fresh material does appear from time to time, so that we cannot omit this well-documented period or attempt to break the chronological continuum from Saxon to modern times.

Before the Normans were victorious at Hastings, the Anglo-Saxons had crossed Offa's Dyke in its mid- and south-eastern sector, and after Hastings the Normans, in turn, established temporary castles against the Welsh, and soon entered Welsh territory. The motte and bailey castle is well-known, but some details require attention. The motte itself was usually flat-topped to provide a foundation platform on which to erect a timber keep. The entire unit was often surrounded by a wide ditch. Such castle mottes were a feature in Normandy before the Conquest, and are depicted on the Bayeux Tapestry. In fact, Edward the Confessor, who was known to have Norman sympathies which paved the way for Harold's defeat, invited Norman builders to construct some in this country, especially at Richard's Castle on the Hereford/ Shropshire border within the area of our field study. But after the Conquest, while the new 'landowners' were discussing the local aspects in detail, a broad scatter of these more hastily erected defence points were set up. They were little more than forward temporary block-houses with stockaded timber towers, providing local security points. The bitter struggle between the new Lords of the Marches and the Welsh is well reflected in the wide distribution of such mounds of the motte and bailey group to be found over the area. Before the present survey had been undertaken, many had already been recorded, and others erroneously mapped as 'tumuli' (Figure 13). The corrections made in the field are noted in the Inventory.

The siting of such mottes follows a recognised procedure. They are generally found near to crucial points in the local environment, such as at river crossings, or by important roads or junctions. The Normans from past experience were careful to choose only Marcher Lords of unswerving loyalty to the Crown, and, with this background in mind, the interim motte and bailey network came into being.

The earth mottes of these temporary 'blockhouses' must now be considered from the field reconnaissance angle. Their size is so obvious that they are usually marked on the maps. Some of the castle mounds are to be found in the middle of a village, and, indeed, very close to the church. It is often quite difficult for a large 'tumulus' or burial mound to be distinguished from the castle type. If a bailey is present or recognisable, the position is conclusive, and this should at the outset be determined. But, in Wales, in particular, some never had a bailey; their absence thus proves nothing. The next approach, therefore, should be to look for an access route, which would naturally be well-worn and, therefore, discernible as a hollow track, even after weathering and in-filling over the centuries. Tracks connecting the mound to a nearby water supply could also be sought. Again, as mentioned above, the top of the mound is usually flat for a castle, to provide the platform on which to build the keep. The name of the field in which a mound stands, or perhaps an adjacent wood, may bear some castle reference. In such cases, it is unlikely to be a burial mound. Finally, some mounds are of natural formation, perhaps of morainic origin, which may have been scarped in order to suit their natural profile to an acceptable defensive rôle. Thus, in some instances, the situation is easily discernible without recourse to excavation.

As decisions were made as to the location of permanent residences of the feudal lords for the areas, so the permanent stone-built castles were erected, and the area under review is marked by a north to south chain of them on a

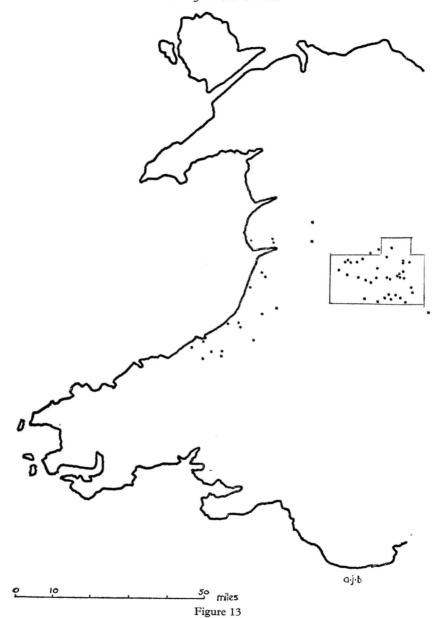

a·j·b

0        10                                    50    miles

Figure 13
Sketch map of motte sites.

similar course to that of the earlier Offa's Dyke, as at Welshpool, Montgomery, Bishop's Castle, Clun and Knighton.

While the majority of stone-built castles are plotted correctly, and most of their respective histories published, again it is only ancillary material for which search was made and recorded. Three farm houses were visited in the Clun Valley which were known to be associated with the activities of the lords of Clun Castle. These are as follows :—

(a) The Lower Spoad (SO 257821) has in its kitchen a massive oak quarter-beam chimney-breast carved with a primitive hunting scene (Fig. 14). The beam could have been carved by the keeper or verderer of Norman times. The carving combines a fine pictorial hunting scene with a very primitive rendering of the hind transfixed by an out-size arrow, so reminiscent of the prehistoric Lascaux cave paintings. The depicting of both stag- and boar-hounds must have given the unknown artist-carver immense pleasure in recording the highlights of the sport for which he lived, as well as gratification to the Lords of the castle and their retinue as they rested and feasted at this stage of the chase.

(b) Moor Hall, (SO 216818) further west, contains a most interesting old staircase. In its newel-post is a recess containing a spear-rack, while under the stairs the space is enclosed by a grill, and was used to confine the hounds while the hunters had a meal. This is a convincing piece of evidence that Moor Hall was also closely associated with the activities based on Clun castle. Moor Hall does not stand on the present main road which is quite recent, but on the original road into the forest.

(c) A third farmhouse, Hall of the Forest SO (208836), is today a modern building on the south side of the road, but opposite is a substantial mound, known locally as the 'Hospital'. When re-visited in August 1974, it was found to have been cut through, and only about a third of it remains. The word 'Hospital' is intriguing, as it suggests a connection with a place of refuge from the Latin word, *hospitium*.

The connection between the three farmhouses is difficult to prove, yet all three are unrecorded antiquities. It may, however, be that they constitute a chain of hunting lodges interspersed westwards alongside the old road from Clun castle into the Clun Forest game reserve. There is an interesting local tradition that Hall of the Forest was where the ladies of the hunting parties stayed. It was once known as 'Ladies' Hall'. They were no doubt fatigued

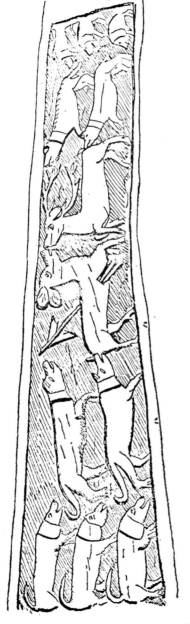

Figure 14
Spoad chimney-breast carved beam.

on reaching that distance from the castle, while their more energetic menfolk could press on with the hunt further westwards into the more difficult terrain and rejoin them later.

A farmhouse, probably connected with Clun castle, and known as Villa Farm, just northwards out of Clun on the side of the main road to Bishop's Castle, has in its north wall the remains of three Norman windows, while adjoining the west wall is a large mound. It is possible that under this mound lie the remains of the main block of the original house of Norman times. It is also likely that it was the Priest's house belonging to the castle. The tradition of an underground passage between here and the castle is discussed in detail in a later chapter (Ch. X).

While the study area is ringed by an impressive complex of abbey foundations, such as Shrewsbury, Wenlock, Buildwas, Valle Crucis, Strata Marcella, Cymmer, Talley and Strata Florida, only Abbey Cwm-hir in Radnorshire falls directly within it. Documentation will supply information on the structure and histories of each, especially relevant to the Norman Period. Awareness of their influence upon the area should be appreciated by the field worker, in view of the fact that communications between them would cross the area, and that ancillary information is pertinent.

In order to clarify the economic background to the Cistercian Abbey of Cwm-hir, founded in 1176, it will be seen from the accompanying map (Fig. 15) how widespread were the granges, and how great was the extent of the lands belonging to such a remote establishment. The Cistercian Order was the most powerful in Wales, and the monks were extremely capable as 'business executives', quick to exploit the latest agricultural techniques, and *au fait* in the marketing of produce in the greatest demand. Thus, like other Cistercian houses sheep-breeding and wool production was the mainstay at Cwm-hir. Where better than the uplands of Radnorshire for this purpose with a proportion of land in the lower river valleys of the Severn, Wye and Teme for the production of arable crops. Its economy would seem to present a favourable picture in its earlier years; but it would seem to have never recovered from the Glyn Dŵr raids at the dawn of the 15th century.

Of interest to the field worker is the fact that many of the Cistercian granges were very similar to small monasteries, in that they had chapels and accommodation facilities for monks and lay brothers, though this was not so in every instance. As a result of the Black Death, the employment of lay brethren had to be replaced by paid servants, and the increase in monastic expenditure thus incurred resulted in the granges and their farms being leased out, instead of being administered from the monastery. Another interesting feature shown by the grange map is the distribution and the disposition of the granges in relation to the 800 ft. contour. Generally speaking, the river valley examples represent the '*hendre*', where the livestock were wintered, while those above that contour represent the '*hafod*' where the stock were taken in the summer to allow cultivation to be undertaken. The areas occupied by the granges could offer a wide opportunity for field research, especially for remains or evidence of chapels, or accommodation buildings occupied by lay brethren. This could be a most valuable addition to the O.S. Map of *Monastic Britain* (South Sheet), as is invited in the Foreword to the folder containing this map by the Director General.

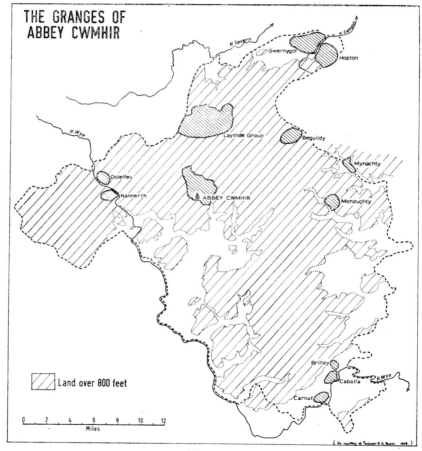

Figure 15

Inter-connecting road systems are known, as, for example, the present Ford Street in Clun, which was once known as 'Frog Street'. At SO 222919 in the Chapel Meadow, where the present farmhouse of Gwern-y-go stands, was the successor of one of the Abbey's grange farms of which only its cellars survive. At SO 239686, the farm of Monaughty is dated 1636, and is probably built from the grange farm of Mynachdy, a mile away to the north-west. The site of Mynachdy (SO 230696) was still visible at the end of 1956. It measures 120 yards by 60 yards (131 m. by 65.6 m.) with a 12 ft. (3.35 m.) shallow moat fed from the Cwm Byr stream. It remained as a grange farm until the Dissolution in 1536, when activities were transferred to Monaughty.

As regards the churches of the period within the area, their history, as far as is known, has usually been recorded in local publications and guides, and once again special features alone need attention. Among these, reported in the Inventory, are such as the site of the deserted church and settlement at Goreham and at Burfield, to which reference has already been made above; there are also the fast-disappearing foundations of the Norman church at Upper Snead, near Bishop's Castle to the west. The wood craftsman's skill of the times still survives in the roodscreens, as at Old Radnor and Llananno in Radnorshire, probably carved and fitted into the churches *in situ*, and not, as the guide books claim, having been brought from Abbey Cwm-hir after the Dissolution; Llanwnog, too, in Montgomeryshire, and Betws-y-crwyn in Shropshire have very fine examples. The impressive air of antiquity still pervades the scene in the remains of Norman arches surviving in church structures, as at Llanbadarn Fawr in Radnorshire. Though but a shadow of their original form, they can be incorporated with earlier Saxon herring-bone masonry or perhaps with later Transitional or Early English features to form the present-day amalgam of styles. Clun church is such an example; here the churchyard is round and thus thought to carry a prehistoric tradition. A charnel-house has been found in recent times, and here the yew-trees are thought to have been flourishing when the Normans were building. Many church towers remind one forcibly of fortress keeps, as, indeed, they were so used in emergencies throughout the Marches. In the main, it would seem that the parish churches, at least those which form part of the Norman heritage, were built from stone extracted from local quarries. The exigencies of local labour and transport resources would virtually render this imperative. A special study in itself could be most rewarding, if the actual quarry used for each could be identified before it is too late. In the same way, many houses in the area are sited near to a quarry from which the stone of which they were built was derived.

## Chapter X

# THE DROVERS' HIGHWAYS AND THE CONTEMPORARY RURAL SCENE

A MAJOR activity of far-reaching importance to the region under review is that of the Welsh Cattle Drovers. The ramifications of this enterprise created highly important contributions, both to the economic and financial structure of the Principality, and, indeed, of Britain in general.

In the 1940's came the realisation of an important link in the chain of the drovers' history. The recognition of a complex system of earthworks near the Anchor on the Shropshire-Montgomeryshire border was made, representing what appeared to be a cattle-shoeing pound (SO 178820) and grading enclosures (Fig. 16). If authenticated, it will prove to be one of the most easterly locations for shoeing cattle before they descended to the lowlands, from mid-Wales to the feeding pastures of the East Midlands, and the fairs of London and the South-east. Diaries and documents on the drovers' activities are to be found in the National Library of Wales. This 600-year old story of a major feature in the economic life of Wales was dimmed and extinguished by the advent of the railways and, latterly, by the road transport of livestock.

The appearance of a Drovers' road, as in a straightforward line it traverses the high ground, and crosses river courses at definite fording points, is quite pronounced. It is quite often flanked by a high-mounded bank, wide enough for the drovers to ride along on horseback, and from such a vantage point they could more easily control the movement of the cattle. Where such roads are metalled and in use today, a wide grass verge to either side is the feature in open country, but this is not present as the road descends the river terraces. Bitterness among local stockfarmers was, indeed, justified when they learned of the approach of a drove of cattle, which quite often 'absorbed' some of their own stock in passing, before they could confine them securely. The Drovers had regular points, where they could rest and graze their cattle overnight, and some of these places still bear such names as 'The Harp Piece' (from the shape of the Welsh harp) or 'Welshman's Meadow'. Quite a number of inns still bear names associated with the Cattle Drovers, for example, "The Pound Inn,' "The Drovers' Arms" and the "Dun Cow" where the drovers themselves stayed overnight, after the landlords had removed their own valuables from the sleeping quarters !

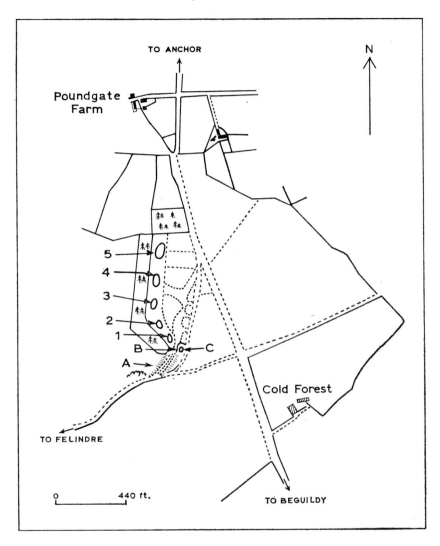

NOTES AND SUGGESTED INTERPRETATION OF THE CATTLE POUND
PLAN (Fig. 16)

The Anchor to Onibury ridgeway runs N.W. to S.E. a mile to the east.

Many fields east of the pound contain old paddock boundary embankments into which the shod or sorted cattle were put.

The lane from Felindre over the river Teme is sunken like the others in the area; this is typical of a Drovers' Way.

A.   The approach sunken way with terraced embankments on either side.
B.   Constricted entrance to allow only one beast to pass at a time.
C.   Probable shoeing-pen depression.
        Depressions 1-4 probably represent the Drovers' quarters, while the
     large one (no. 5) was for the horses.
        It is just possible that the old thorn bushes on the perimeter bank of the
     compound are the remains of an earlier stockade.

Equally important to agriculture were the communication links between the
farming areas and the outside world. The Drovers used, wholly or in part,
prehistoric ridgeways, as well as those of their own making. The coachroads,
too, formed part of the rural scene, and should not be totally ignored. They
were used by the drovers for their return journeys. Along them passed the
traffic in mail and merchandise over the centuries, as well as the landlords
from their Welsh estates to the cities, especially to London. By mutual
arrangement, the drovers would pay the rents of Welsh farmers to London-
based landlords out of proceeds from the sale of cattle. They would even
bring back to their womenfolk the latest London dress fashions, where they
would often be seen long before they reached the English Provinces. The
London to Aberystwyth coachroad crosses the area, entering at the east over
the ford at Halford, near Craven Arms, and as many records of the original
milestones, as have been found, are shown in the Inventory. Other features,
too, have been noted, including coaching inns and cock-fighting pits. Cock-
fighting was a recreation typical of these Drover days, when the audience
gathered around a pit in which two contestants placed a cock which fought its
rival to the death. Needless to say, the winner secured a prize for its owner,
and gambling was an added attraction. Parts of this coachroad are in use
today, while others are now overgrown, or merely rutted headland cart-tracks
across fields, or used as Forestry Commission rides.

Incidental to the general drovers' road pattern, there emerged from the
fieldwork the sites of overgrown early roads leading to villages. A number have
been obliterated or diverted by country estates, notably Walcot at SO 342843
and 335860, and Bedstone at SO 344898 and 368757, both in Shropshire.

Farming activities and customs, familiar to the early drovers, have been
noted in passing, and there are many in such a rural setting. They ranged
from the cultivated platforms on the terraced lynchets on the limestone of
South Shropshire and North Herefordshire to the shallow earthwork boundaries of the 'quillets', (where pigs were permitted to forage for acorns and
beechmast,) to the disused buildings where once the blacksmith and wheelwright served the community, as well as to strip-field cultivation areas. An
illustrative concentration of some of these early agricultural activities is shown
on the following map (Fig. 17), bordering a main drovers' route in North

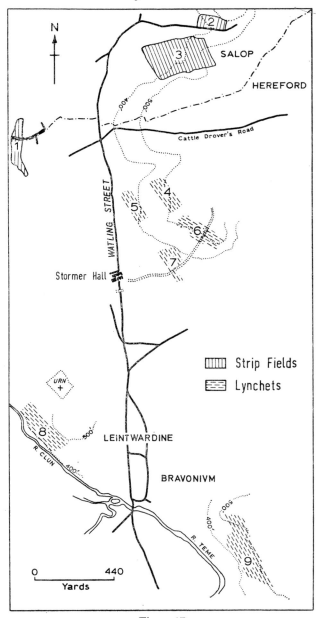

Figure 17

NOTES ON THE MAP OF EARLY AGRICULTURE (Fig. 17)

The map of this limestone area of North Herefordshire shows a concentration of agricultural features which not only lie on either side of the Roman Watling Street, north and south of BRAVONIUM, but also to either side of the Drovers' Road. The Roman road, in the upper section of the map, is mainly a footpath in grass fields. Stormer Hall was built across its track, and in the orchard to the south, (shown by two small dotted lines), a sample excavation had been made in June 1953, which had revealed a cobbled road surface 6 inches below the turf, in which traffic ruts showed a 5 ft. span of axle. The thickness of the road material averaged one foot.

MEDIAEVAL COMMON FIELDS (Strips).
     No. 1   area contained 17 strips
     No. 2   area contained 8 strips.
     No. 3   area contained 17 strips.

LYNCHETS.
     Nos. 4 & 5 are indistinct, but probably comprise some 10 terraces.

     No. 6   is a set of 5, about 190-200 yards long and terminating on N.W. in a transverse bank. The terraces vary in width, but are in fair condition. They were in later times traversed by a track.

     No. 7   is a set of 6 terraces (again traversed by the same track). On the east side of the site is a square flat earth 'platform' in fair condition.

     No. 8   These lynchets represent workings on the river terraces. They consist of 5 terraces 200-215 yds. long, the outer ones being 17-23 yds. wide, and the intermediate one is 4 yds. wide. Another 5 continuing N.W. are 160-180 yds. long and 16 yds. wide, except for the second from the top which is 5 yds. wide. All are in good condition.

     No. 9   This comprises 6 terraces 190-200 yds. long by 4-12 yds. wide. The vertical height of these varies from 10-15 ft. They continue a little further S.E. being a repetition of a further 6 of the same length.

It should also be noted that, in the field marked 'URN', was found the handle of a Romano-British urn (native ware) in October 1953, and later verified by the National Museum of Wales, Cardiff. Two flint flakes were also found in the same field.


Herefordshire. The occasional water-mill and corn-mill are best traced through old documents. Even those occupations, found in this rural setting and absorbing the local labour requirements, are included here as being part of the background—the brick-kilns, stone quarries and the tile quarries, lest they become misinterpreted in later years.

Another note-worthy feature of this area is the old cottage which was part of the rural scene over 200 years ago. Quite a number have been found which had beaten earth floors, originally covered with rushes. In passing, one should note where former crafts were carried out in a settlement, such as those of the wheelwrights and blacksmiths. There are also many examples of habitations, or their remains, standing in a narrow slang of land or enclosure bordering the lanes or roads. These are generally "squatters' " houses which can hark back to around the 16th century. They were quickly erected on the margins of waste ground belonging to estate lands. One excellent example of these (at SO 274835), not far to the east of Offa's Dyke (where the author lived for twenty years), is known as Lane House at Mardu (Fig. 18). It was originally built in the early 15th century with one room on the ground floor from which an upper room was reached by ladder through a trapdoor. A small pantry was added in 1550 with wattle and daub interior walling. The interesting custom was that the occupier had to pay a squatters' fee of one shilling per annum to Lord Powys. This was redeemed by the writer's family in 1940 by paying one guinea, representing 21 years.

Figure 18

Lane House, Mardu, near. Clun—an example of 'squatters' cottage (16th. C.), modified later; site of Whitby jet bead behind trees above left house chimney; prehistoric habitation site on ridge above horizon slanting hedge; stray flints found on each field in view; house stands at 700 ft. and highest point at 1,000 ft. (left edge of photo) ; stream passes between buildings; a ridgeway traverses top of hill from left to right.

(Photo by Ron McLaren)

## CHAPTER XI

## MAGIC AND RELIGION

IT has been stated earlier that, within the general terms of reference laid down by the Archaeological Branch of the Ordnance Survey, any shred of evidence which might conceivably point to anything of interest topographically and historically, either visually or by hearsay, should be noted on the maps as a record. As a field recorder, the author developed the experience that there were many factors which in different ways focussed interest on each individual spot. The earlier text and the subsequent Inventory have portrayed the extensive and varied material which came to light visually in the course of the work.

But it was found that the complete absence of visual ground evidence is in no way conclusive against the existence of a site. As is shown by some of the records in the Inventory, there were quite often several reasons why attention was focussed upon a particular place.

The main corpus of the work is founded upon visual and documentary evidence, but it was found that there was one aspect which, although circumstantial in itself, either had a bearing on, or could point to, archaeological evidence. This type of approach includes local folk-lore, which could preserve traditions about localities. These traditions had been handed down from the dim past through many generations, albeit embellished and exaggerated over the years, but, nevertheless, they were for the most part grounded in fact.

Experience showed that it was on the Welsh/English Border that the major concentration of folk-lore anecdotes was found, no doubt fostered by the location of these parts within the zone of continual struggle between the Highland and Lowland folk in their efforts to defend their habitat. Thus, the evolution of the culture of this Border country developed around suspicion, and, in an effort to instil wariness and fear of an invader, the inhabitants would tend towards exaggeration in recounting earlier happenings. This was accentuated by the very limited population dispersion and lack of travelling facilities with consequent in-breeding.

A particular feature encountered in the fieldwork was the study of wells (Fig. 19). Holy wells, of course, are related to religious beliefs, and the benefits accruing to each well were proportionate to the depth of each indi-

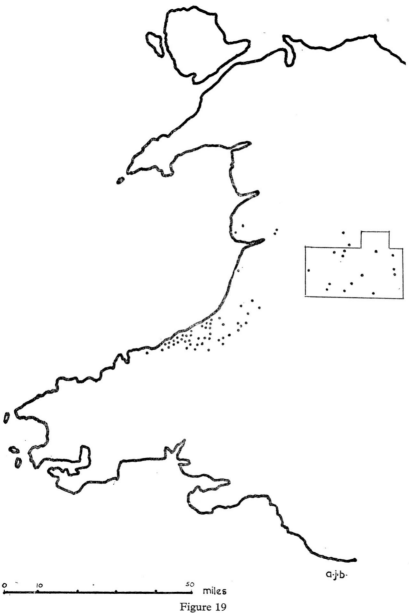

Figure 19
Sketch map of holy and healing wells (sites).

vidual's belief or faith. These wells were claimed to have medicinal or healing properties, often due to the different kinds of minerals in their waters in solution from the rocks through which they welled to the surface. In these instances, the water was either taken orally or applied externally to affected parts of the body, as in the case of eye complaints. Furthermore, there is a substantial group of wells outside the 'holy' group, such as the chalybeate ones with curative properties. Many have been recorded on O.S. maps, and were thus interpreted as falling within my terms of reference. In pursuance of this, the work of Francis Jones was fully consulted prior to visiting the sites recorded by him or those on maps. The thoroughness of his research is fully acknowledged. However, as it transpired, there were still quite a number to be rediscovered before being lost for ever beneath the inroads of land development, and a considerable amount of up-to-date information on present-day conditions and deterioration seemed imperative. The result was that a number of wells belonging to all three groups can be added. The type of research employed is illustrated by the example of 'Jackets Well', near Knighton at SO 278718, which seems to suggest a possible corruption of the Welsh word for 'healing'—*iachâd*.

A well of any group is, in a sense, a tangible object, visible in the field, and is evidence on the ground of a culture which was often absorbed by Christianity without any real breach in continuity from Pagan or Celtic religious life. Primitive rites and beliefs were adapted to Christian usages for the purpose of directing the faltering steps of doubting Britons on to the road to Salvation. Survivals of pre-Christian cults are still in evidence in this area, especially in the remoter localities, where outside influences have not too forcibly penetrated. The recording of these distorted echoes of the past should, indeed, be made, because within each, it is believed, lie the seeds of historical or archaeological facts, however fossilised or disintegrated they have become.

In the middle of the village of Aston-on-Clun, west of Craven Arms, on the B4368 road, is an old aspen tree (*Populus tremula* L.), on the branches of which are fixed every May Day a number of flags for decoration. Before the introduction of the Gregorian Calendar, there were recognised but two seasons in the Celtic year. As the leaves took on their autumn tints, from green to russet brown, and were shed from the trees, so the onset of winter dormancy and nature's hibernation was accepted by everyone, and the date of this event was stabilised around 1st November (Calan Gaeaf). When, in due course, nature emerged from this dormancy and re-clothed itself in foliage, this was spring, and the date was fixed around 1st May (Calan Mai). Thus, there were only these two seasons in the Celtic pre-Christian calendar, and the concept itself was a survival from earlier pagan ideas. Christianity eventually usurped the Spring Festival by introducing Easter, based on the Resurrection of the Dead, and everything associated with or ascribed to re-creation. Other traditional 'celebrations' around early November were associated with fires, which persist today as Guy Fawkes Night bonfires and fireworks on the 5th, which in turn might be correlated with the tidying up of the rural scene by burning the hedge-trimmings and waste vegetation of field and garden. At the onset of winter, too, there is the veneration of the last sheaf of corn harvested, the 'Corn Dolly', and All Hallow's Eve, to name but a few customs.

The decoration of this 'Arbor Tree' is clearly associated with the survival of some pre-Christian custom associated again in turn with the resuscitation of the natural vegetation.

Other customs, both economic and social, gathered around this festival. Country activities awakened at that date with the custom of transhumance from the *hendre* to the *hafod*, that local migration of man and beast from the lowland to the upland pastures. There were also the hiring fairs of May Day and 1st November.

By the very nature of research into legend and folk traditions, a wide variety of notes is accumulated, which do not fall easily into clearly defined categories. Although the 'Giant's Cave' (SO 316993) is the local legendary site of King Arthur's resting place, the stone (SO 348891) is supposed to turn round whenever the clock strikes thirteen ! The associations with Arthur and his twelve Knights are very tenuous. The same stone is also claimed to have been thrown by the Devil from his 'chair' on the Stiperstones. Whereas the giant of the cave just mentioned might refer to Arthur himself, the giant of the legend at SO 420800 who stood on View Edge opposite to a second one on Norton Camp would seem to be different. These two were employing the services of a raven to guard the key to their treasure hidden in Stokesay Pool ! Such large men might be a memory of the Saxons in the minds of the Celtic people of lesser stature.

Woodgate (SO 310953) was the meeting place of witches, and would seem to hark back to the activities of those who worked the prehistoric axe factory around Corndon Hill, using the local picrite rock. Two white cows are also featured, and apart from the more familiar one associated with Mitchell's Fold stone circle, the second one appears at SO 283916 haunting Pentre Wood, where Mrs. T. Hatfield, nearby, claimed to have seen it in 1955 ! One can conceivably correlate the white cow with the Wild White Cattle, whose survival persists today in the Chillingham, Cadzow, Chartley, Dynevor and

Vaynol herds, and whose progenitors would be the native cattle of prehistoric times (*Bos longifrons*). The colour is unblemished and, indeed, a royal prerogative, as is noted in the horses, or white chargers, ridden by Kings and Princes throughout history.

Border legends are very common, as is well illustrated by Charlotte Burne, notably 'The Roaring Bull of Bagbury'. The 'Bagbury Bridge' alluded to in it is at SO 318933. . References to animals continue also in the Black Dog which haunts Aston Dingle (SO 299914) at midnight, where Mr. Williams, near the Pentre, claims to have seen it in 1955. Others speak of violent death around here. Yet, the 'Dog and Duck' (SO 268895) was originally a public inn on the coachroad, so named from the then prevalent sport of baiting ducks on the pond. This is a recent tradition, retrieved before being obscured by time. But it is not so in the case of an underground passage between Villa Farm and Clun Castle (SO 299812), where local folk-lore claimed that whoever tried to pass along it was obstructed by a closed door. The door was 'booby-trapped' by a guillotine blade which maimed the hand that tried to lift the latch. The river Clun passes between the castle and the house, and, if, indeed, there is an underground passage, then it would more likely be for drainage from house to river, with a second passage from the castle to the river.

There is a traditional battle-site at SN 951770, while another at SO 109744 states that at the Soldiers' Well combatants washed their wounds after a battle in Battle Field (Banc y sidi at SO 105742).

Although all the material in this Chapter is very fractionated by reason of its very nature, nevertheless, these traditions which survive in the countryside should not be overlooked, nor turned aside merely from the fact that they represent matters such as popular etymology, and observations for which there is no proper historical record. Items of folk-history, crumbs though they are, should still have their right and proper place on the lord's table.

"These observations are, I trust, true on the whole, though I do not pretend that they are perfectly void of mistake, or that a more nice observer might not make many additions, since subjects of this kind are inexhaustible".

Gilbert White (1720-1793).

# INVENTORY

-----

The counties are in alphabetical order, Hereford, Montgomery, Radnor and Shropshire.

The Ordnance Survey (O.S.) maps referred to are the County series on a scale of 6 inches = 1 mile. Each sheet is a quadrant of the full sheet, arranged from north to south for each county. The quadrants are in the accepted order of NW, NE, SW, & SE. Sheets which overlap one, two or three county boundaries also bear O.S. numbering of one, two or three county numbers, as the case may be. This is illustrated on the Location Map Index in Figure 1.

Each record bears a six-figure National Grid Reference Number, so that, if the new 1:10,560 or Six-inch National Grid Series or the 1:25,000 ($2\frac{1}{2}''$ = 1 mile) sheets are used, site locations can be readily identified. For example, a reference of SO 497328, by taking the first and fourth figures of 4 & 3, would indicate that this reference appears on $2\frac{1}{2}''$ sheet number SO 43. Also by noting where it lies on this sheet, it can be ascertained in which quadrant of the 6″ scale map it appears. In this instance, therefore, the eastings 497 line lies to the eastern edge of the map, and the northing 328 is a little north of the base of the map; the northing and easting lines thus intersect in the SE quadrant, so that the number of the relevant 6″ Nat. Grid sheet is SO 43 SE.

In each record entry, one word at least is in italics to emphasise the subject of the record for the reader.

N.B. In the absence of a comprehensive publication for Shropshire of an authoritative status, the interpretation of the origins or meanings of place-names in this study area is offered only as an exploratory basis for the etymologist. In each case, they are quoted from local verbal contacts.

HEREFORDSHIRE :

1   SO 398744   2 S.E.

In the area between the river Clun and the 500′ contour are *lynchets* (possibly modified river terraces) at 100 yds. N.E. of the river and 750 yds. W.N.W. of the church; they consist of 5 terraces 200-215 yds. long ; the outer ones are 23-17 yds. wide and the intermediate one is 4 yds. A second group of 5 terraces immediately to the N.W. measures 160-180 yds. long and 16 yds. wide, except the second from the top which is 5 yds. wide. All are in fairly good condition.

2   SO 393740   2 S.E.

The two *mounds* above and below this grid are not tumuli, they are glacial fluvial material being the residual parts of the 25′ gravel terrace. Both are stratified gravel. They are not drumlins which are purely glacial.

3   SO 404743   2 S.E.

Just S. of the chapel have been found two possible *Roman querns,* with the report of a third found nearby.

4   SO 411735   2 S.E.

E. of Trippleton from the 600′ contour W. to the lane are six *lynchet* terraces 190-200 yds. long by 4-12 yds. wide with vertical height of 10-15 ft. Also to the S.E. of them is a second series of 3 terraces of the same length. All are in fairly good condition. They are on the limestone.

5   SO 401725   2 S.E.

In the N. corner of Brandon Camp three *flint flakes* were found by D. G. Bayliss in 1955.

MONTGOMERYSHIRE :

6   SJ 248088   23 N.E.

Regarding the *place-name* Buttington, the *Anglo-Saxon Chronicle* states that in 894 A.D. the English levies overtook the Danes at 'Buttingtune'.

7   SJ 246089   23 N.E.

Buttington Bridge is an important *crossing* of the Severn. Tracks lead to it from both sides. (ford, before there was a bridge)

8   SJ 250088   23 N.E.

There are traces of a rectangular *earthwork* where the church and the school now stand. It may once have controlled the crossing here of the Severn.

9   SJ 249084   23 N.E.

N.W. from School House along the W. side of the stream, *Offa's Dyke* appears as a raised ridge.

10   SJ  250078   23 N.E.
>     *Offa's Dyke* is now nearly ploughed out at this point.

11   SJ  249076   23 N.E.
>     The *hollow-way* here was deepened in the 19th C. to ease the gradient. An
>     original gap was probably here, curving S.W. from the well (marked on the
>     map) through the Dyke. It is 30 yds. S. of the present hollow-way. It is
>     seen as a field depression where the original track went.

12   SJ  225076   23 N.E.
>     Opposite St. Mary's church door is Maen Llôg, a *prehistoric altarstone*
>     subsequently used as the throne of the Abbot of Strata Marcella, the
>     Cistercian monastery nearby. 3 miles N.E.

13   SJ  248064   23 S.E.
>     Adjacent to the N. wall of the farm building, the map shows the scarp of
>     *Offa's Dyke* to swing about 20° from the N. to S. alignment, but this is
>     really the steep scarp of the natural flank of the valley. The ditch and bank
>     of Offa's Dyke are definitely traceable in continuous alignment on the
>     valley floor N. of the building. S. of this farm building to the letter 'O' of
>     'Offa's', the ancient trackway has preserved the W. ditch of the Dyke.
>     The ploughed-down bank is traceable and should be so noted on the map.

14   SJ  247059   23 S.E.
>     At the 'Q' of 'Quarry', the scarp is 27 ft. high. At 200 yds. S. there is a
>     deep *hollow-way*.

15   SJ  248056   23 S.E.
>     From the N. end of the wood due S. for 500 yds. the line of *Offa's Dyke* is
>     seen here as a scarped berm or platform, and was discovered by Sir Cyril
>     Fox. Thereafter it is evident for 140 yds. and again fades out for 450 yds.

16   SJ  275070   24 N.W.
>     To the S. the Long Mountain *ridgeway* enters from the Hope Gap in the W.
>     and leaves at the Shropshire border. It then proceeds through Westbury
>     to the Mercian kingdom, linking up with the Roman road to Wroxeter. On
>     it at grid ref. 2808 is the Welsh Harp, the meeting-place of ancient track-
>     ways on the Long Mountain.

17   SJ  278070   24 N.W.
>     The more westerly of the two *tumuli* is 80 yds. in circumference, 6 ft. high
>     and 27 yds. in diameter. The other smaller one to the E. is only 24 yds. in
>     diameter and has a shallow trench across it (possibly due to interference).
>     It is 35 yds. from the summit of the one to that of the other.

18  SJ 253048  24 S.W.
   *Offa's Dyke* re-commences here at the head of the ravine which has been
   used in the interval.

19  SJ 251042  24 S.W.
   This gap in the continuation of *Offa's Dyke* (where it crosses the 800′
   contour figures on the map) is in fact traceable, and should be shown on
   the map, as it is on the 1836 1″ O.S. sheet no. 60.

20  SJ 248034  30 N.E.
   The portion of *Offa's Dyke* in Green Wood is being damaged by periodical
   timber felling. Just S. of the Lodge, the Long Mountain *ridgeway* appears
   as a hollow-way in its course to the lowlands, and its subsequent straight
   line may possibly be due to the Dyke being thrown up on the line of the
   *Roman Road* from Westbury to Caer and the river Severn, though not
   proved by excavation. The opening at the 4th milestone N. of Court
   House is the earlier road crossing gap.

21  SJ 238014  30 N.E.
   Caer is a *Roman fort* of Flavian date, occupied from 1st to 3rd C. It was
   probably Lavobrinta (*vide Arch. Camb.* vol. xciii, 1949).

22  SO 246984  30 S.E.
   The *castle mound* at Winsbury is moated.

23  SO 245974  30 S.E.
   The *castle mound* at Dudston is moated.

24  SO 207984  30 S.E.
   At Rhyd Whyman was the *ancient crossing* of the Severn river.

25  SO 213980  30 S.E.
   This *motte and bailey* is the original castle site of Roger de Montgomery.

26  SO 225989  30 S.E.
   In the S.E. corner adjoining the W. side of the main road are the ruins of
   an old *brick-kiln.*

27  SO 230999  30 S.E.
   From this point at the S.W. corner of the wood, the unrecorded track of
   *Offa's Dyke* passes the B.M. 273·7, (Pound House) in a straight line S.S.E.
   to SO 232989, following the field boundaries all the way.

28  SO 234978  30 S.E.
   From the S.W. corner of Rownal Covert, *Offa's Dyke* follows the two field
   boundaries S.S.E. to the main road and the S. edge of the map, with an
   original gap for the road.

29  SN 963965   35 N.W.

Caer Noddfa *Roman Camp* is rectangular 300 ft. by 200 ft. The valla have been considerably altered and have disappeared on the site of the church. A huge *carn*, it is said, was once in its centre from which over 1,000 (sic) loads of stone were removed for fencing and road purposes. In 1909, a trial dig revealed a V-shaped ditch of Roman type. The camp stands on the line of the *Roman road* which ran W. up the valley; a portion of this road is visible on the W. side of the main road, running N.W. from the 'Aleppo Merchant' Inn, and was formerly known as 'Sarn'.

30  SO 043975   35 N.E.

This old *road* coming S. from Court Farm, Heath Farm and by Ffrwd wen was probably used by *monks* from Strata Florida. It is not very clear today, but probably linked up with the Roman road coming N. from Caersws and is itself not likely to be Roman.

31  SO 050970   35 N.E.

This point is the S.W. corner of an area surrounded by footpaths (also overlapping onto Mont. sheet 36 N.W.) which represents the track of a ditch. Celynog was a *grange* farm Strata Florida, but its site is unknown. In 1638 it was 'meered round and surrounded by a two-faced ditch called the "Abbot's Ditche'. This may be an earthwork antedating the monks' grange.

32  SO 045955   35 N.E.

The *Roman road* was once called 'Sarn Sws' (from Caersws).

33  SN 983915   35 S.W.

On the S. edge of the map is a *standing stone* which is $5\frac{1}{2}$ ft. high, $2\frac{1}{2}$ ft. thick and 3 ft. wide, with no signs of any inscription on it.

34  SO 023945   35 S.E.

This defensive *earthwork's* outer rampart is 6 ft. external height, 12 ft. internal fall. The ditch averages 6 ft. The inner bank is similar, but lower towards the E. After 140 ft., there is a break in both banks; the outer bank continues at lower level for nearly 30 ft. when it appears to join another bank running down the hill for 80-90 ft. Caersws Roman station is visible $1\frac{1}{2}$ miles to the S.

35  SO 030920   35 S.E.

Caersws Roman *Fort* was Mediolanum.

36  SO 073966   36 N.W.

The second and third *fields* S. of Fir House are called Lower and Upper Cae Castell. There is now no indication of a '*castell*' being extant.

37  SO 076952  36 N.W.
Gareg lwyd was formerly called Ty'n yr wtra. The *place-name* may point to a vanished site.

38  SO 080954  36 N.W.
Gareg lwyd *boundary stone* stands at the junction of the parishes of Aberhafesp, Tregynon and Betws Cedewain. An inscription on it (viz. EEITLLL) probably represents the initials of the churchwardens of the three parishes (E.E. ; I.T. ; and Ll.L. or L.Ll.) which were inscribed on it at some unrecorded perambulation of the parochial bounds.

39  SO 123968  36 N.E.
The present village water supply was once a *holy well* called 'Pistyll can pwll' close to Betws church.

40  SO 122967  36 N.E.
Behind the school in the field called Maes y Domen was once a large *mound*, but it has now been removed.

41  SO 106974  36 N.E.
The *field* in which the word 'Bridge' is printed is called 'Cae maen', which suggests a lost *stone* somewhere.

42  SO 108965  36 N.E.
There are no remains of pavement or *causeway* at Waun Sarnau on the road to Caersws from Betws Cedewain.

43  SO 128946  36 N.E.
The two parallel *dykes* are each 6 ft. from the bottom of the external ditch to the top of the crest. There is 25 ft. between them. They stretch 250 yds. S.W. from the farm which obliterates the line and travel E. towards Cloddiau.

44  SO 061943  36 S.W.
There is a possibility of there being a *wayside cross* at Bryn y groes.

45  SO 087940  36 S.W.
Black *well* was only *chalybeate*, with no evidence of it ever being a holy well.

46  SO 073922  36 S.W.
Under the word 'Newtown', the mound is a *tumulus* 18 ft. high and 130 yds. in circumference. There is a record of a Mr. Proctor who (about 1850, from a verbal report from Newtown Public Library) remembers his grandfather digging this mound from the summit; he discovered human bones and a few bronze implements. Although the finds cannot now be located, the summit does actually show signs of disturbance, as well as near to the base.

47   SO  108914   36 S.E.
>    A *holy well*, 'The Old Lady's Well', still existed in 1909, but covered in.
>    It is in Lady Well Court Lane stated to be on the site of the Common or
>    Green.

48   SO  107914   36 S.E.
>    The Mound is a *motte and bailey*, the outer earthworks of which have been
>    partly erased by landscape gardens.

49   SO  123933   36 S.E.
>    Gro Tump is an 11th C. *motte and bailey* guarding the ford over the Severn.

50   SO  126925   36 S.E.
>    The Wroxeter-Westbury-Caersws *Roman road* crosses the river at this
>    ford, and then S. following the footpath to St. Giles' Cottage and past the
>    Rectory.

51   SO  133923   36 S.E.
>    This ring of trees has every appearance of making a *tumulus* site.

52   SO  175964   37 N.W.
>    The camp is a *motte and bailey*. It is mentioned in Hulbert's *Antiquities of
>    Shrewsbury* of 1837 that "there are supposed to be the remains of a monas-
>    tery at Castell Goran Ddu, which was destroyed by Henry III".

53   SO  237971   37 N.E.
>    The line of *Offa's Dyke* should continue S. to the footpath at the N. end of
>    Dudston Covert where there is a natural gap of 17 yds. wide, representing
>    an old traffic lane.

54   SO  240962   37 N.E.
>    The scarp of *Offa's Dyke* here is 24 ft. and the W. ditch is 4 to 5 ft.

55   SO  222919   37 S.E.
>    The previous farmhouse of Gwern y go was the monastic *grange farm*
>    belonging to the Cistercian Abbey of Cwmhir. The *field* in which the
>    house stands is the Chapel Meadow. The present cellars are ancient, and
>    probably survive from the grange.

56   SN  970910   42 N.W.
>    The boggy tract here is known by the *place-name* of Sarn y glyn.

57   SN  974911   42 N.W.
>    The *standing stone* is not inscribed; it is 6½ft. high, 2½ft. wide and 2½ft.
>    deep. The *field* in which it stands is called Cae y garreg.

58  SN 965906   42 N.W.

A number of *stones* around Birchen House are thought to have come from the *Roman Road*, but would seem to be too large.

59  SN 970906   42 N.W.

There are 2 unrecorded *meini hirion*. The large stone, now the main gatepost to the farmyard of Church House, was in the 19th C. removed from the parish churchyard where it also served as a gatepost until the churchyard boundary was removed. It is 78 ins. high above ground, tapering upwards, and 47 ins. in girth halfway up. Near to this, in the same farmyard, is another; square topped 5 ft. high and 6 ft. in girth. A circular hole is drilled on one side. The origin of this is unknown.

60  SO 028904   42 N.E.

The *field* which contains the windpump N. of Llandinam Hall is known as Cae Domen ( =the field of the *mound*), but so far, there is no indication of a mound.

61  SO 029891   42 N.E.

There are indications of a *mound* (Cae Domen) in the grounds of Plasdinam to the N.W., but the present lay-out of the College property has effaced its character.

62  SO 046904 42 N.E.

The *motte* is 45 ft. high and 175 ft. in circumference at ground level ; the moat is 25 ft. wide and 12 ft. deep.

63  SO 050910   42 N.E.

This is the old *ridgeway* (see record no. 66).

64  SO 053913   42 N.E.

This *motte* is about 30 ft. high and 30 ft. diameter at the summit. (N.B. the *ridgeway* passes in front of it on its way up the hill). This mound compares closely with the opposite mound at Aberhafesp (mound on the N. side of the Severn).

65  SO 035854   42 S.E.

In 1910 this *cairn* was reported as being completely destroyed due to the wire fences intersecting the site. It was roughly circular and 25 ft. in diameter, but in *Arch. Camb.* of 1868 (III), vol. xiv, p. 23 it is described as an oblong mound 13 yds. by 5 yds. by 1 yd. in height.

66  SO 049868   42 S.E.

This is an ancient mountain *ridgeway* from Caersws in the N. via Giant's

Grave, by Polin Groes Du, through Bwlch y sarnau, by Abbey Cwmhir and to Llandrindod, (see record no. 63).

67   SO 044861   42 S.E.

The Giant's Grave is probably a *cross-dyke* athwart the ridgeway. It is a ditch with a dyke on either side, the one on the N. being of greater height and breadth than the S. one. The ditch is 3 ft. deep. It is actually extended from the moor down to one of the feeders of the Finnant brook down the sides of Nant y Dygwm—i.e. about 200 ft. further S. than the map stippling shows.

68   SO 015877   42 S.E.

Gaer farmhouse and buildings stand inside the area of a former *earthwork*. Most features of the camp have disappeared, but there are traces on either side of the house. That part on the W. side and behind is 30 ft. long and 3 ft. high.

69   SO 082909   43 N.W.

This *field* W. of Middle Scafell and N. of the road is called Cae Domen. Though there is no indication of a *tumulus*, it may have some bearing on the unrecorded mound further E. at Brynhyfryd.

70   SO 088910   43 N.W.

On the 91 grid line and adjoining the road, is a *mound* which appears to be a *tumulus*.

71   SO 102909   43 N.W.

The road follows the course of the *Roman road* over the Park Brickyard and Glan Hafren, about 1 mile W.

72   SO 100908   43 N.W.

In 1874, between the road and the railway, a *flint axehead and flake* were found 40 yds. from the turnpike and N. of the railway. They are now in Welshpool Museum.

73   SO 088885   43 N.W.

In the E. corner of the second field N. of Glascoed is a *mound* which may be of archaeological interest.

74   SO 132908   43 N.E.

The field (in which Yew Tree Cottage is in the S.W. corner) contains 2 *stones*—one central 100 ft. S. of the N. boundary, and the other about 60 ft. along the boundary from the S.E. corner in the hedge. At the N.W. corner, the small oval 900′ contour has no noticeable earthwork.

75   SO 150902   43 N.E.

This *tumulus* is smaller than its neighbour in the same field eastwards.

76   SO 140861   43 S.E.

The Kerry Hill *ridgeway* crosses from the E. in S.W. direction to the S. edge. Sir Cyril Fox's interpretation of this ridgeway (as the distribution of Short Dykes indicates) points to it and its extensions as forming the chief route of raiding highlanders, there being 9 (out of 16) connecting with it. The Dyke, too, is strongest in this area. The ridgeway hardly changes level (100 ft. at the most) over 7 miles of broken country, and is the main way from the highlands over the best fords (Halford on the Onny and Quatford on the Severn) to the lowlands, aiming at Tamworth, the capital of Mercia.

77   SO 117851   43 S.E.

The W. *tumulus* is 6 ft. high, 80 yds. in circumference and is flat topped.

78   SO 118852   43 S.E.

The E. *tumulus* is 8 ft. high, 95 yds. in circumference, 30 yds. in diameter and is flat topped.

79   SO 102857  &  SO 116850 43 S.E.

The Cross Dykes, also known as Double Deyches, are immediately pre-Offan. They are in effect a *cross-ridge dyke* athwart the Kerry Hill ridgeway and the divergent tracks. The boggy ground (itself a defence) of the sources of the rivers Mule, Teme and Ithon lie between the W. and E. portions. Both have the same alignment and are one complete work; the technique is so similar to the W. ditch and high counterscarp that Fox considers that the gang who built this work went on later to construct the Hergan section of Offa's Dyke over the Salop border. The W. portion is 630 yds. long; the E. portion is ½ mile long with an 8 ft. deep ditch, following the curve of the hill. It should continue 370 yds. still further E. than the map shows. These 'Double Deyches' may represent the last localised effort at defence prior to being superseded by the 'agreed frontier' of Offa's Dyke.

80   SO 102857   43 S.E.

The 3 *tumuli* just N. of the Dyke are correct, the S. one is 30 yds. in diameter.

81   SO 143873   43 S.E.

The mound shown here is a *tumulus*.

82   SO 149870   43 S.E.

These are probably *earthworks* of archaeological significance.

83   SO 145866   43 S.E.

Road widening here by the Forestry Commission had in June 1955 skimmed off about ¼ of the E. edge of this *tumulus*. It is 60 yds. in circumference and is 8 ft. high.

84   SO  107858   43 S.E.
The mound at the S.W. corner of the triangular wood is probably a *tumulus.*

85   SO  104903   44 N.W.
Towards the N.W., runs *Wantyn Dike,* which is a cross-valley dike (Mule-Caebitra)—a western end of fertile valleys. This is a protective screen in front of (i.e. W. of) agriculturally developed areas of lowland, identical in alignment technique to Offa's Dyke. It is thus likely to be of Mercian construction against the highland people.

86   SN  958846   48 N.W.
On Lower Green was once *a holy well* called Ffynnon Idloes.

87   SN  958794   48 S.W.
The narrow second *field* S. of Tan y berth is called Garreg lwyd, but there is no evidence of any antiquity. The field name may be only topographical from the hill-name or the nearby old quarry.

88   SO  043789   48 S.E.
Fowler's Horse Block is a *natural outcrop* of rock 60 ins. above ground and 800 ft. from the S.E. point of the circle.

89   SO  042792   48 S.E.
Fowler's Arm-Chair *stone circle* is $3\frac{1}{2}$ ft. above ground and is the centre stone of which 6 stones are visible (5 are just so, and the 6th about 1 ft. above ground). The 6th stone is due N. of the centre one. Going E. round the circle, the next 3 stones are 5 yds. apart from each other; then blank for 64 yds. to the 5th which is due W. of the centre; then 15ft to the 6th, and back again 15ft. to the N. stone. From the circle to the base of the *cairn* is 20 yds. This cairn is much disturbed and about 2 ft. high with a base circumference of 150 ft. of local loose stones.

90   SO  018805   48 S.E.
This *tumulus* was in the 19th C. 70 yds. in circumference and 7 ft. high, but now reduced.

91   SO  024813   48 S.E.
This *tumulus* is a low mound 56 yds. in circumference and 3 ft. high. It has been heightened by a 9 ft. high triangulation mound and a hole dug in which to erect a 30 ft. pole many years ago—about 1880, or earlier. A skull and human bones were found and re-interred.

92   SO  043804   48 S.E.
At the back of Newhouse are possible remains of *ramparts.* They are called 'camp' on the Tithe Map.

93  SO  112821   49 N.E.

This *tumulus* is known as 'Dickey's Stool'. It is 250 ft. in circumference and 4 ft. high. The diameter on the N-S axis of the summit is 66 ft. and flatter than Domen Ddu at Abbey Cwmhir. It is in Llanbadarn Fynydd parish.

94  SO  102817   49 N.E.

There is no trace of a *cairn* as the name Garn implies, nor on Garn bryn llwyd to the N.

95  SO  111841   49 N.E.

A mound here has every appearance of being a much spread *tumulus*. The centre is 145 yds. N.E. from B.M. 1530·77 on the gatepost and 48yds. due E. from the post and wire fence road boundary. Its apparent diameter is 24 yds., but the circumference of the original is indistinct, but appreciable.

96  SO  142833   49 N.E.

The *camp* entrance was probably on the E. side; it is rather a pastoral than a defensive earthwork. It is similar to that at Poundgate on Radnor sheet 5 N.W. The best preserved section is on the W. in the plantation, which is 5 ft. high with a 4 ft. wide ditch. It is about 500 ft. in circumference.

97  SO  112822   49 N.E.

The western *tumulus* of the pair is 190 ft. in circumference and 4 ft. high; it is in good preservation and untampered with. It is in Beguildy parish.

98  SO  113822   49 N.E.

The eastern *tumulus* of the pair is 200 ft. in circumference and 4 ft. high. It appears to have been interfered with; the wire fence at the trackway passes over its S. perimeter. It is in Beguildy parish.

99  SO  112831   49 N.E.

This unrecorded *tumulus* is flat topped and of the same structure as the many tumuli hereabouts. It is 74 yds. due E. of the road to its W. perimeter. Diameter is 60 ft. and height 6 ft.; circumference is 198 ft. No reason to suspect interference.

100  SO  113825   49 N.E.

This unrecorded *tumulus* is 5 ft. high, 30 yds. diameter and 110 yds. in circumference. It is spread towards the E. It lies 46 yds. N.E. of the N. point of the pool with which it aligns at the corner post of the field boundary fence. This post is 191 yds. from its centre. It is also on a straight line between the field fence centre to S.E. and the above tumulus in record no. 99.

101  SO  067844   49 N.W.

Tomen Bryn-dadleu (or Bryn Dadl) is almost circular and 12 ft. high

(about 20 ft. on the S.E. bank of the stream) and 77 ft. diameter on the
N-S axis, and 3 ft. wider E. to W.  It is about 100 ft. long and appears to be
a *motte*.

102   SO  112848   49 N.E.
The track from the N., passing S.W. over the road B4355 and the Cider
House is the Kerry Hill *ridgeway*.  It then goes W. to Abbey Cwmhir,
St. Harmon, Cwm Deuddwr to Ystrad Meurig and the coast in Ceredigion.
It was the London coachroad in more recent times.

103   SO  129833   49 N.E.
Lluest *farmhouse* is half-timbered (see record no. 106 for a possible association).

104   SO  107841   49 N.E.
This *tumulus* is conical, but circular.

105   SO  117827   49 N.E.
Windy Hall is a modified *Welsh longhouse*.

106   SO  125830   49 N.E.
To the N. of 'Ford' is a mound which appears as a small *motte* with slight
outer earthworks.

107   SN  959770   52 N.W.
The W. *earthwork* of the two Cwm y Saeson is crescent-shaped, 3 ft. above
the surrounding level, 60 ft. long and 50 ft. between the terminals.

108   SN  961770   52 N.W.
The E. *earthwork* of the two Cwm y Saeson is oval with 6 ft. wide entrance
on the stream side adjoining.  It is 60 ft. long and 36 ft. wide and 6 ft. high.
The enclosed area is 4 ft. higher than the outside field level.  No local
traditions associated with either earthwork.

109   SN  964775   52 N.W.
This *tumulus* has been ploughed, but is 6 ft. high and 225 ft. in circumference, and though a little lower than originally, it is otherwise undisturbed.

110   SN  963775   52 N.W.
Originally there were 8 *standing stones* in the field Cae garreg, but they were
removed about 1890, 7 of them being used to preserve the banks of the
Dulas from erosion, and the 8th used for farm purposes.  They appear to
have stood in line E. to W. on a low mound 90 ft. long and 20 ft. wide, all
facing N.  Those in the river bank are about 7' by 3' by 2'.  The holes from
which they were removed were visible in 1911.

111 SN 973781 52 N.W.

Allt-lwyd is a late 17*th* C. *stone house* of two stories, rectangular and with a tiled roof. The kitchen floor is of patterned pebble pitching.

112 SN 967777 52 N.W.

The Soldier's Grave is a low mound on which traces of 2 small *barrows* could be seen in 1911. It is 80 ft. in circumference, 3 ft. high and oval in shape.

113 SN 964776 52 N.W.

The *standing stone* is over 8 ft. high out of the ground and 40 ins. across. Its broad faces are to the N. and S. and 30 ins. thick. It is the largest extant stone of an original group of 5 arranged in a quadrangle called 'Daufraich a dau law'.

RADNORSHIRE :
114 SO 056806 4 S.W.

This holding was known as the 'Maens'. It was verbally reported to me that about 1850 there existed a low boulder *standing stone* about 4 ft. high which used to be called 'the Maen stone'. It was solitary, but is not now traceable.

115 SO 058795 4 S.W.

Regarding Pantygroes, although no evidence or records confirm it, the *cross* (groes) may have some ecclesiastical significance with its proximity to a *holy well* (David's well).

116 SO 060786 4 S.W.

David's Well (a *holy and healing well*) was much frequented for its medicinal properties. The water flows through a pipe into a stone-lined trough 3 ft. wide and 4 ft. deep. The Water contains sulphur. The Welsh name is Ffynnon Dafydd y Gof. The district takes its name from the well.

117 SO 085786 4 S.W.

There is no evidence of any *cairn* in any of the meadows at Dolygarn as the name would imply.

118 SO 130800 4 S.E.

In the N.E. angle of this grid ref. on the N. bank of Trefoel Brook, some *Roman pottery* of the 1st to 2nd C. was found by Frank Noble (of Knighton School) in 1956.

119 SO 140800 4 S.E.

In the N.E. angle of this grid ref. are some 'shepherds' *enclosures* forming a square of ditches and banks.

120   SO 130794   4 S.E.
      This *tumulus* which probably gave the name to Gareg Lwyd hill, is flat
      topped, 210 ft. base circumference, 6 ft. high and grass-covered. It shows
      signs of being opened on the E. side.

121   SO 120793   4 S.E.
      This track which comes down from Fron Top and along past the ruined
      cottage of Castle Tump is the *mountain road* from Llanbadarn Fynydd to
      Felindre.

122   SO 124798   4 S.E.
      Castell y blaidd is a horse-shoe shaped *earthwork* 610 ft. long and 24 ft.
      high with ditch all round 6 ft. wide and 5 ft. deep. The ends of the rampart
      are 75 ft. apart. It is known locally as Castle Tump from which the ruined
      cottage is named.

123   SO 101790   4 S.E.
      This field E. of the road and below the printed word 'weir' contains a flat-
      topped (comparable with local types) *tumulus*. The flat top is 21 ft. diameter
      and is 15 ft. high. Adjoining the lane in the N.W. corner of the same field
      is a small banked enclosure 12 yds. by 14 yds., with base circumference of
      400 ft. It was discovered by Christopher J. Bird in August, 1956.

124   SO 116786   4 S.E.
      Llymwynt is referred to locally as the site of an *old church*, and a stone
      piscina and capital have been brought down to Llanbadarn Fynydd church
      porch. The place was burned down by the children of the last occupier
      named George about 1919, one of whom lives at the Moat. But in R.C.A.M.
      Radnorshire 1913, it is referred to as "The venerable mansion called Llyn-
      went" (no. 262, p. 66) much of which was taken down in 1782, but sculp-
      tured freestone and fine timbers and stone capitals are of a date before 1563
      when it was the residence of the Radnor High Sheriff. It was the home of
      the ancient family of the Vaughans and Merediths, and should be spelt
      Llynwent = Llyn Gwent, because Gwent is the correct name of the brook.

125   SO 217801   5 S.E.
      This is the find-spot of a decorated *spindle-whorl* found by Norman Ellis of
      Little Selly about 1950. There are four identical C-shaped curves arranged
      around the central hole. It is in Clun Museum.

126   SO 013782   8 N.E.
      On the lintel of the door of this small *cottage* Prysgduon is the date 1711
      and the initials R.W. It is also known as Presdeion.

127   SO 017783   8 N.E.
      Of these 2 *tumuli*, domen ddu is 12 ft. high and 270 ft. circumference; it is

disturbed on the E. and W. sides. The second one called the 'Mound' at 20 yds. N. of this is 3 ft. high, flat topped and 225 ft. in circumference.

128  SO 006756  8 N.E.

This mound, known locally as 'the Domen', may be artificial, though it appears as a *tumulus* 250 ft. circumference, 5 ft. high on N. side and 10 ft. on the S. side.

129  SO 011755  8 N.E.

This *tumulus*—the Mount or Bedd Garmon—is 8 ft. high and 270 ft. in circumference.

130  SO 039732  8 S.E.

In the field called Rhos, the site of a former *tumulus* is oval and 215 ft. in circumference. It is only distinguishable by the soil which is darker brown than that in the rest of the field.

131  SO 040725  8 S.E.

The 3 *fields* between Lower Esgair and Fishpool Farm are all known as Maes Maen, but there is no sign of a *stone* in any.

132  SO 019736  8 S.E.

Only the base of Castell y garn *cairn* now remains. It is 200 ft. in circumference and only 2 ft. high. It has been looted for its stone and crossed by a boundary fence. Reports of white quartz pebbles being seen there among the strewn debris were verbally received.

133  SO 036749  8 S.E.

The *Roman road* from Caersws to Castell Collen probably follows this road as indicated by reports of stone pitching near this quarry, and again by the finger-post in Bwlch y Sarnau.

134  SO 044749  8 S.E.

The 3 small enclosures at the end of the short lane S.W. of Pant y rhedyn is the site of a disappeared *cottage* formerly known as Grey Stone or Garreg lwyd. There may have been a *monolith* nearby.

135  SO 049743  8 S.E.

Saint's Well (within the spinney) is a *holy well*. The spring water rises into a natural stone basin.

136  SO 039742  8 S.E.

The old *farmhouse* of Hên Du, although re-built in the 18th C., has still the original stone chimney stack of the former house.

137   SO 071768   9 N.W.

These *fields* were once a smallholding called Castle, and one of its adjoining fields was called Tŷ'n y Castell. These references no doubt are coupled with Castle Bank which was probably connected as the grazing rights to Castell tinboeth. These pasturing rights still accrue to the occupier of Castell tinboeth ground.

138   SO 090754   9 N.W.

The masonry remains of Castell tinboeth (or Dinbod or Dinbaud)—the Mortimer stronghold—probably occupy the site of a former *hill fortress*, as is suggested by outlying earthwork fragments.

139   SO 051767   9 N.W.

The *place-name* Sarn Dolau-gleision is also known as 'Green Meadow Causey'.

140   SO 095777   9 N.W.

At Tŷ Llwyd, before 1880, a *stone hammerhead* $17\frac{1}{2}$ ins. in circumference and $6\frac{1}{2}$ ins. high and weighing 10 lbs. was found on a local farm not known today. I have traced this hammer-head to be still in possession of Mr. Lewis of Tŷ Llwyd whose father obtained it from the farmer (i.e. the finder) who kept the Post Office (now Rock Villa) in those days. This is the stone referred to in *Radnor* R.C.A.M. No. 251.

141   SO 080769   9 N.W.

The *earthwork* is 100 ft. long, 5 ft. high generally, but 8 ft. high at the N. end. A 6 ft. wide ditch runs down the E. side.

142   SO 121778   9 N.E.

These small *enclosures* around the spring were, according to the Tithe Schedule No. 956, the unit of the now disappeared holding called Castell Cwtta, unknown today, and there is no significant name clue to suggest a camp.

143   SO 141777   9 N.E.

This old track along the parish boundary is a *'green road'*.

144   SO 139780   9 N.E.

This *tumulus* is 6 ft. high and 150 ft. in circumference.

145   SO 144778   9 N.E.

This conspicuous *tumulus* is 10 ft. high, and 320 ft. in circumference. It is conical topped.

146   SO 126769   9 N.E.

This N. *tumulus* is 6 ft. high and 200 ft. in circumference, and heather covered.

147   SO  126768  9 N.E.

This S. *tumulus* is higher at about 8 ft. with 200 ft. circumference, heather covering it.

148   SO  114761  9 N.E.

The Groes is probably not ecclesiastical, but alludes to the cross-roads just to the E. near to the 1312 spot level, where another '*green road*' comes up from Cold Harbour in a N.E. direction over Gorslydan.

149   SO  103778  9 N.E.

The *field name* is Cefn Maen, but there is no evidence of any 'maen' or stone.

150   SO  095744  9 S.W.

The dotted lines within the river Ithon represent the course of the *ford* which is approached at the W. end of the church at Llananno by a pitched causeway of laid and fitted small stone blocks. The church contains the celebrated rood-screen of late 15th C. work, probably carved by craftsmen from Abbey Cwmhir, rather than being a portion of the Abbey screen itself, as it is a complete piece in itself. (see also the screen in Newtown church in Montgomeryshire).

151   SO  123738  9 S.E.

The *field*, in which the spot level 1169 appears, is called Cwm garreg, but there is no trace of a *stone*.

152   SO  099723  9 S.E.

This triangular *field* (second from the W. edge of the map sheet) is called 'Tump Piece'—but this is probably only due to natural features.

153   SO  127734  9 S.E.

At the old *farmhouse* called Upper Cross Cynon there is a cast-iron fireback dated 1649 and an oak cheese-press dairy fixture dated 1706.

154   SO  130733  9 S.E.

At Lower Cross Cynon (originally Croescynon) the spring is said to be slightly medicinal and was formerly known as Ffynnon Gynon, a *healing well*.

155   SO  137725  9 S.E.

Bron y garn lwyd is corrupted now to Vron gan llwyd. There is no trace of a *cairn*.

156   SO  109744  9 S.E.

This spring is known as the *Soldiers' Well*. No relics have been found.

157   SO  109739   9 S.E.

The hollowed-out capital of an Early English *pillar* from Abbey Cwmhir
was found in 1805 at Caer Faelog (see *Radnor* R.C.A.M. no. 263, p. 67.).
It was long used as a trough and is 12 ins. high and 59 ins. in circumference.
The top is hollowed and has a small leaden drainpipe in one side.  It is now
preserved in Llanbister church, where the tower is built at the E. end
owing to its siting on a rocky eminence.  There are Early English remains
in spite of restoration in 1908.

158   SO  145725   9 S.E.

The two roadside *fields* S. of the school and E. of the road are in the Tithe
Schedule as N. Upper Saint Du, and S. Lower Saint Du, but these names
are unknown today; they are called Maes yr hardy from the near-by farm.

159   SO  143723   9 S.E.

Castell coch is the old name of the *motte and bailey castle* of Penlan ½ mile E.
on the Radnor sheet 10 S.W.

160   SO  175768   10 N.W.

These 4 *tumuli* are of the same form and size, low with flattened tops.  All
are of 300 ft. base circumference.  The one at the N.W. end is 6 ft. high, the
next is 10 ft., the third 6 ft. and the one at the S.E. is 5 ft. high.

161   SO  171778   10 N.W.

The *holy well* called Fair Well is a corruption of Mair Well ( = Mary's Well).

162   SO  153763   10 N.W.

This field, W. of the road and the spinney, contains the '*King's Rent Hole*',
an oval hole cut into the slope of the hill with a diameter of 80 ins. on its
longer axis, 60 ins. deep at the back (i.e. the side against the hill), and
sloping to 20 ins. where the trench enters forming an entrance path.  This
trench was 9 ft. long, 2 ft. wide and 1 ft. deep.  It was cleared out annually
for the ancient custom and quaint ceremony on Hilary Monday of bidding
for the collectorship of manorial dues of £19 18s. 7d.  It is fully recorded
in *Radnor* R.C.A.M. 1913.  In August 1956 I saw Mr Lewis of Tŷ Llwyd,
Llanbadarn Fynydd, (then 78 years old) who used to attend this annual
ceremony and knew some of the bidders.  He said that the custom ended in
1920, as the dues were redeemed by Government request.  The site, easily
discernible in 1956, has since been filled in by ploughing and cultivation.

163   SO  151777   10 N.W.

In the paddock adjoining the S. side of the farmyard at Maesgwyn is the
probable site of a *church and burial ground*.  Faint mounds on the surface
of the enclosure are said to be graves.  It was the only Presbyterian Academy
in Wales between 1730 and 1735.

164 SO 151774 10 N.W.
There is a *mound* here which may be of archaeological interest.

165 SO 152770 10 N.W.
This *field* is called Cae Bishop and may have some ecclesiastical significance owing to its relative position with Maesgwyn above (see record no. 163).

166 SO 147763 10 N.W.
Cwm croes may also owe its *name* to some connection with the above Maesgwyn (see record no. 163) and Cae Bishop (see record no. 165).

167 SO 165726 10 S.W.
The *field* N. of Bryngolfa is called the 'Tump', but there is no sign of a *mound*. Bryn Golfa is probably Bryn Gwylfa ( = the hill look-out) no doubt due to a small natural rise formerly existing in this field which has been divided by the hedge from N. to S. at a point to the W. of the footpath.

168 SO 154724 10 S.W.
Penlan is a *motte and bailey castle*, 45 ft. in E. to W. diameter, and 550 ft. at base circumference.

169 SO 150730 10 S.W.
In the S.E. angle of this cross-grid is the Hendy, an example of a very *early* domestic *dwelling*, now ruinous.

170 SO 147739 10 S.W.
There is no clue as to the origin of the *place-name* Painscastle, unless it is a personal name.

171 SO 154745 10 S.W.
The *field* W. of the sharp bend and the foot-bridge of the brook is called Camp meadow. Though there is a 10 ft. deep ridge it appears to be a natural fluvial formation.

172 SO 167744 10 S.W.
These are 2 *tumuli* 30 ft. apart; the W. one is conical, 10 ft. high and 200 ft. circumference, and probably disturbed; the E. one is 8 ft. high and 170 ft. in circumference and undisturbed.

173 SO 169738 10 S.W.
This *tumulus* is rather weathered, but is 6 ft. high and 150 ft. circumference; it has probably been opened on the S. side, though not within the last 100 years.

174 SO 174726 10 S.W.
Two mounds near to the old quarry are *quarry spoil heaps*.

175  SO 226727  10 S.E.
     The *earthwork* called the Gaer is ploughed out, and was barely discernible
     in 1956. Its sides are about 140 ft. each way with rounded corners. The
     highest extant bank is only 18 ins. It is probably manorial in origin owing
     to the find of *coins* in 1814.

176  SO 218718  10 S.E.
     Bailey farmhouse is built on a *motte*.

177  SO 212717  10 S.E.
     Probably a survival of the former swydd *name* of Rhiwallt.

178  SO 219722  10 S.E.
     Immediately N. of the track, there is a small circular *enclosure* here barely
     discernible. This is probably the 'Holy Piece or holey piece', in which
     event it is the '*King's Rent Hole*' for the Welsh swydd of Rhiwallt. (see
     record no. 162).

179  SO 208735  10 S.E.
     For the *place-name* Llangoch, the parish Registers and tombstones give the
     name Llwyn goch.

180  SO 239733  10 S.E.
     Halfway between the printed figure 1000 and grid 24 S of the track, is the
     site of the discovery of the *Gold Torque* found by Mr. Pugh of Cwm
     Jenkin in 1955.

181  SO 242732  10 S.E.
     This is the site where a *sword* of c. 1400 A.D. was found (*vide Rads. Soc.
     Trans.* of 1954).

182  SO 240724  10 S.E.
     On Bailey Hill, Mr. Thomas Lloyd of Bailey House found 3 perforated
     *spindle-whorls* in a round shallow basin in which was black earth. They
     were ploughed up in the 19th C. Two were lost, but one was seen in June
     1911.

183  SO 233689  17 N.E.
     This camp is a *promontory fortress* (see Radnor R.C.A.M. no. 48).

184  SO 239686  17 N.E.
     Monaughty is dated 1636, and is probably built from the Cistercian
     *monastic* grange of Monachdy, 1 mile to the N.

185  SO 213704  17 N.E.
     The *mounds* here cover the ruins of Weston Hall which was the centre of

the Welsh swydd of Rhiwallt. The chieftain here collected his monetary dues, being the King's Rent, obtained at the ceremony in the 'King's Rent Hole' on Fron Goch hill (see record no. 177).

186  SO 236698  17 N.E.
This *field* (with the printed 900 ft. contour in it) is called 'Church Way Field.'

187  SO 212713  17 N.E.
In the church burial ground is an *altar tomb* bearing the decayed coat-of-arms of Thomas Holland (d. 1764), the last occupier of the now disappeared Weston Hall (see record no. 185).

188  SO 226714  17 N.E.
The *field name* Erw garreg shows no trace of any stones, if ever there were any.

189  SO 230697  17 N.E.
The site of Monachdy was, in September 1956, still visible. It is 120 yds. by 60 yds. A shallow moat 12 ft. wide was probably fed from the Cwm Byr stream. In the S.W. corner are possible traces of small house foundations. It is almost certainly a *grange* of Abbey Cwmhir and removed at the Dissolution to Monaughty.

SHROPSHIRE

190  SO 274999  47 S.W.
This is not a tumulus in the S. corner of the field, S.E. of Hockleton farm, but a *motte and bailey castle*.

191  SO 282005  47 S.W.
From the N. edge of the map, E. of the Old Shafts, is a *ridgeway* which leaves the S. edge at Hagley.

192  SO 278975  47 S.W.
Under the printed 'H' of 'Hagley', adjoining the orchard, is an unrecorded *motte*.

193  SO 273985  47 S.W.
In Eyton's *Salopia Antiqua* vol. xi, p. 69, Whittery ($\frac{1}{2}$ mile N. of Marrington Hall) is Witentreu (Domesday Hundred), possibly a place of *folk mote*.

194  SO 259985  47 S.W.
Chirbury *castle* was excavated in 1953. Its type is uncertain.

195   SO 316993   47 S.E.
Giant's cave; (see Ch. X).

196   SO 320977 47 S.E.
There are possible remains of a Drovers' *Cattle Pound* in this wood, unless they are some remains of lead mining activity.

197   SO 303984   47 S.E.
I have, by probing with an auger, found what may be a central stone in situ at Mitchell's Fold *stone circle*. It is grown over with turf.

198   SO 304983   47 S.E.
This stone circle should be amended to damaged *cairn*.

199   SO 325002   47 S.E.
The *place-name* Hemford = Hên Ffordd—the old road.

200   SO 252954   54 N.W.
'Mount', the so-called tumulus, is actually a *motte* with a slight fosse about 2 ft. deep on the E. side. It is scarped from the natural hill (the record has been amended on the new O.S. edition).

201   SO 285949   54 N.W.
At Old Church Stoke is a 'Lady well' or *holy well*. In former times, it was dressed with flowers and rushes, and pins were thrown into it; people sat round it eating cakes and drinking sugared water. It was dressed on Holy Thursday.

202   SO 325945   54 N.E.
Cf. the *place-name* of Pultheley with Pwllheli.

203   SO 325955   54 N.E.
The *place-name* Runnis = yr ynys (island).

204   SO 300967   54 N.E.
In the W. angle of the triangle of paths is an unrecorded round *barrow*.

205   SO 306956   54 N.E.
New House was formerly 'Michael's House' on the old Ordnance Map; cf. Mitchell's Fold stone circle—a *place-name* change.

206   SO 310953   54 N.E.
Woodgate is immediately below an outcrop of picrite rock from which the Hyssington Type XII stone axes were made; the *axe factory site* has so far eluded identification; several tracks meet here.

207 SO 313943  54 N.E.

On Bryn Bank, which is a small rocky plateau a few feet above the roadway, are signs of a *cockpit* circle; it is also the site of mediaeval festivities.

208 SO 257912  54 S.W.

This *road* is later than the Dyke as the deflection at the crossing shows. Turning S., the road here runs in the W. ditch, and at spot-level 616 cuts into the scarp of Offa's Dyke. N. of Offa's Dyke Cottage, the W. ditch is filled in.

209 SO 248939  54 S.W.

*Offa's Dyke* is levelled here, but a definite hump is visible. Further S., just N. of Brompton Hall, the W. ditch is ploughed in.

210 SO 251932  54 S.W.

*Offa's Dyke* is visible in the orchard and garden of the Blue Bell Inn. The tumulus so marked S. of the Blue Bell garden appears to be a *motte and bailey castle*. The Dyke here is not scheduled officially; I reported damage by lorries removing stone on 6th September 1954. The Dyke alignment appears to pass to the W. side of the motte and bailey castle.

211 SO 253925  54 S.W.

N. of Mellington Wood, the *Dyke* is much spread in boggy ground.

212 SO 260917  54 S.W.

Oldhall Cottage is the centre of the *Domesday vill Muletune*, and is the site of old Mellington Hall.

213 SO 343915  54 S.E.

In the wall of a roadside building, opposite the N.E. margin of the circular churchyard, is a stone laid lengthwise on edge, which is 5 ft. long and $2\frac{1}{2}$ ft. in width above ground. The shape suggests a *megalith*.

214 SO 329925  54 S.E.

In the S.E. corner of the field, just under the printed B.M. 618·7, is a possible *tumulus*.

215 SO 326932  54 S.E.

S. of the E. end of the track that runs E. to W., is a large mound which is more likely to be a *motte* than a tumulus.

216 SO 299914  54 S.E.

At the S. end of the field near to the road and to the E. of the Dingle, is the site of a *tumulus* which was levelled by T. E. Parry Jones, the owner-occupier in 1942, by removing a few cart-loads of top soil and stones off the apex, and spreading them round about. The cist is probably not destroyed. A crop of oats in 1955 showed a darker colour than the surrounding growth.

217   SO 334910   54 S.E.
The so-called tumulus to the W. of Lydham Mill should be *motte and bailey castle*; it has since been amended on later O.S. editions.

218   SO 938296   54 S.E.
The *field* at Newhouse Lane and W. of the footpath to the edge of the sheet is known as the 'Battlefield'.

219   SO 309929   54 S.E.
The field S.W. of Upper Snead contains at the N. corner the dressed stone *foundations* of a Norman church still visible. It is unploughable.

220   SO 311924   54 S.E.
The *field* in which Upper Snead Bridge appears is called the "Friars Field" or "Prior's Field". An outcrop at the E. corner is also called "Friars Field or Prior's Rock". (see records nos. 219 and 221).

221   SO 313917   54 S.E.
At Owlbury the *conventual buildings* of a former monastery are still extant and incorporated.

222   SO 305915   54 S.E.
The site of the Owlbury *brickworks* was only a pool in 1954.

223   SO 352914   55 S.W.
In the N.W. corner of the field, S. of the road and opposite to the S.E. corner of the Avenue, a ground eminence has every appearance of being a *tumulus*.

224   SO 350935   55 S.W.
The 'Butts' represents the site where the men at arms of the Lords of More used to practice with the *long-bow*.

225   SO 366928   55 S.W.
There are traces of *earthworks* around the house and buildings. These are referred to in Auden's *Little Guide to Shropshire*, p. 75.

226   SO 388923   55 S.W.
This saline spring was in use as a *healing well* up to about 1900. It is the cure for blood disorders and for rheumatism (information supplied by T. Jones, Mardu in 1956).

227   SO 212878   61 N.E.
The Kerry Hill *ridgeway* enters this S. edge of the map (it is called 'the

Sarn') and leaves the E. edge at Pantglas. It was also the old London coachroad from Newtown, Kerry, Sarn, 'Dog and Duck', Bishop's Moat, Kerry Lane, Bishop's Castle, Stank Lane to Craven Arms.

228   SO 238889   61 N.E.

This has been a large *round barrow*—now planted with firs and much spread. Visited by Miss L. F. Chitty 10/8/28.

229   SO 207897   61 N.E.

This so-called 'tomen' is a *motte and bailey castle.*

230   SO 203890   61 N.E.

For *Wantyn Dyke,* see record no. 85.

231   SO 214884   61 N.E.

At this point about 300 ft. S.E. of the northern stream is an unrecorded *mound,* slightly oval, much spread due to deep ploughing by the Forestry Commission.

232   SO 222880   61 N.E.

Sir Cyril Fox connects the Lower *Short Dyke* with Offa's Dyke; it is a lowland people's work thrown athwart the ridgeway against the hill people, as the ditch on the W. side denotes. This is one of 8 similar works W. of Offa's Dyke, and is one of 5 placed athwart an important pre-Offan ridgeway. It represents a local effort at defence and consolidation in the immediate pre-Offan period.

233   SO 188872   61 S.W.

These *boundary stones* were not visible in 1956, and may have been removed by the Forestry Commission in planting or road works.

234   SO 175868   61 S.W.

A *flint arrowhead* was found here in 1930 by H. N. Jerman.

235   SO 182863   61 S.W.

The three fields S.W. and the one N.E. between the road and the Rhuddwr Brook are continually yielding *flint artefacts* on ploughing. Found by Mrs. Moody, formerly of the Anchor Inn.

236   SO 196863   61 S.W.

*Flint chippings* have been found here.

237   SO 192867   61 S.W.

The S. end of the Upper *Short Ditch* has been ploughed out in the two upper enclosures for 300 yds; this is also pre-Offan as is record no. 232.

238   SO  188867   61 S.W.

Bettws Grange is also known as Croes y sarnau; *placename* =cross-roads.

239   SO  198869   61 S.W.

The Kerry Hill *ridgeway* enters the E. edge of the map here and proceeds W. via Kerry Pole Cottage to SO 150863.

240   SO  158861   61 S.W.

This area contains the site of a lost *stone circle*. In *Mont. Coll.* 1889, vol. xxiii,. p. 82, the writer states:—'In N.E. direction, a straight line for 300-400 yds. towards Kerry Pole House. It was not found by R.C.A.M. in June 1909. It has only 6 stones remaining and suggests a circle. It is indicated by a central stone with the position and distance of 3 others. The remaining ones are thrown out of the circle, all of which are at irregular distances : (23ft., 20ft. 4ins., 18ft., 54ft. 6ins. and 19ft). A possible unknown site of a third circle is at SO 15828612.

241   SO  158861   61 S.W.

The Kerry Hill *stone circle* comprises 8 stones surrounding a central 9th. The E. and W. ones are set up edgewise to the centre one; the others present a flat face. They vary from 37 ft. to 45 ft. from the centre, and from each other they vary from 27½ ft. to 35 ft. round the perimeter. (see record no. 240).

242   SO  193848   61 S.W.

At this spot, a Bronze Age barbed and tanged *arrowhead* was found by G. Jones of Weal's Old House. It is now in Clun Museum.

243   SO  165852   61 S.W.

The mounds S. of the road opposite Old Quarries may be *quarry spoil* rather than *earthworks*.

244   SO  169862   61 S.W.

This mound is almost certainly *quarry spoil*. The interior was examined in 1951 by myself when the Forestry Commission removed a portion for use as road metal.

245   SO  170852   61 S.W.

Here is a very likely ploughed-out *barrow* just to the E. of Gloddfa Nursery, as observed by Miss L. F. Chitty.

246   SO  175847   61 S.W.

This road, via the Anchor Inn, Kerry Pole and Hilltop farm footpath, is the Springhill *ridgeway* on which many antiquities of the Stone Age have been discovered as far as Bromfield to the S.

247  SO 156875  61 S.W.

At Windy Hall, a large ochreous *flint scraper* was found in the garden in 1948 by John Fletcher Jr. of the Rhespass. It is not likely to have been *in situ*, but picked up as a curio by an earlier occupier.

248  SO 166866  61 S.W.

This *tumulus* is 45 yds. in circumference and 6 ft. high. It shows signs of interference.

249  SO 152863  61 S.W.

This *tumulus* is 6 ft. high well preserved.

250  SO 158862  61 S.W.

This shallow *tumulus* is known as 'Shenton's Tump.' (see Fig. 4). A ploughed-out lost tumulus is shown on an air photograph at SO 162861.

251  SO 153862  61 S.W.

*Flint implements* have been found here.

252  SO 155860  61 S.W.

At this spot a *flint and a spindle-whorl* were found in 1935.

253  SO 159851  61 S.W.

Just below the 'w' of 'fedw' on the W. bank of the stream, are unrecorded earthworks which appear to be old *field systems*.

254  SO 245848  61 S.E.

On this boundary, on 19th February 1950, an *Iron Age spearhead* was found; it is probably Early Iron Age, but it may be up to, but not later than, Roman. It is ribbed, with solid socket. It was examined and preserved by W. F. Grimes, at the London Museum.

255  SO 240850  61 S.E.

'Roman' camp is very doubtful indeed. It is probably a *village site* of Welsh highlanders during a period of Mercian pressure. There is the site of a 14 ft. diameter bastion at the junction of the two antennae-like earthworks, 21 yds. from which is a 250 yds. long hollow-way, itself being ploughed in November 1955 and badly spread. Within the camp is a cross-shaped hollow 71 yds. from the N.W. corner. Overgrown in the bracken are two lines of stones running S.W. nearly to the footpath, the N. line being of larger stones than those in the S. one.

256  SO 245876  61 S.E.

Above the 'd' of 'Round' was found a small flat stone with the date of 1716 on it. Also delineated on it, cut in the stone, was the boundary of the property, the initials of the owners, and the site of the house, garden and the approach road to it. Also on it was a cross orientated to the Pole Star.

The stone is local Old Red Sandstone and is in possession of the owner, F. B. Davies, of Newcastle Mill. It is thought to be a primitive *property deed inscribed on stone.*

257 SO 244868 61 S.E.
Surface finds of *flint implements* have been obtained in both fields.

258 SO 225878 61 S.E.
The prehistoric 'Irish' *ridgeway* enters the top edge of the map and leaves the E. edge at 246862. But note that the parish boundary probably follows the original line of the ridgeway, and that at about 300 yds. due E. of Two Crosses farm a deep sunken way (about 500 yds. long) is the original route on the E. side of the present road.

259 SO 240868 61 S.E.
In the S.E. angle of the 5-road junction (exactly where the B.M. 1511·2 is printed), an aerial photograph by Dr. St. Joseph shows an ovate ring. On the ground, a depression 2 ft. deep with a rather stony embankment is bare of vegetation surrounded by a profuse growth of rushes. It is either (a) the remains of a *dewpond* or (b) a decayed *pound* for stray cattle.

260 SO 206854 61 S.E.
Outside the point of the right-angle bend of the footpath is a solitary rowan tree, and proceeding W. along the N. side of the path are 5 small *stones* set *upright*: no. 1 is 38 yds. from this tree; no. 2 is 70 yds. from no. 1 and is $2\frac{1}{2}$ ft. high; no. 3 is very low 30″ wide and 56 yds. from no. 2, but just on S. edge of path; no. 4 is 180 yds. from no. 3, and no. 5 is 35 yds. from no. 4. They appear to be a *boundary* mark, possibly the remains of part of the boundary of the old townships of Ruthen and Ruganthen. (see Hearth Tax Roll of 1672). On the S. side of the path, between the 'R' & 'h' of printed 'Rhos' is a ground depression.

261 SO 212878 61 S.E.
The Kerry Hill *ridgeway* passes from the N. edge of the map to 198869, this section being called Yr Hên Ffordd.

262 SO 203869 61 S.E.
The Cantlin *Stone* marks the spot where a pedlar in 1691 was found robbed and dead. When this land was in dispute during the Enclosures of 1875, Betws y crwyn parish claimed it because it had buried this pedlar in its churchyard. He was only known as William, and 'C' was added to signify 'Can't tell' what his surname was; 'Can't tell' was later corrupted to Cantlin.

263 SO 198863 61 S.E.
Riddings, and Railground at SO 205863, probably represent Ruthen and Ruganthen *townships* as incorporated in the Hearth Tax Roll of 1672 (see record no. 260).

264  SO 206856  61 S.E.
     An oblong *stone* 18 ins. square stands here at the source of a small stream
     flowing N.W. to B.M. 1306·3.

265  SO 273897  62 N.W.
     Sir Cyril Fox attributes this *camp* called Caer Din to the Dark Ages; the
     *ridgeway* was deflected to pass through it as a sunken hollow-way.  The
     camp represents Mercian military activities of the pre-Offan period in the
     ebb and flow of debated frontier, and Offa's Dyke was the final agreed
     boundary.  The camp is no doubt a plateau fort used as a village settlement
     of Welsh highlanders during the Mercian pressure.

266  SO 268894  62 N.W.
     The *field* N. of Pwll y piad is the site of Mainstone Wakes which ceased
     sometime about 1870.

267  SO 261889  62 N.W.
     The lane from Edenhope passes through a gap in the *Dyke*.

268  SO 263887  62 N.W.
     The gap in *Offa's Dyke* is 11 yds. wide.

269  SO 263883  62 N.W.
     Just S. of this *ridgeway* is an original gap, denoting a deflection in the road.

270  SO 272892  62 N.W.
     The *placename* 'Garden' is an obvious corruption of Gaer Din.

271  SO 219896  62 N.W.
     Bishop's Moat is a fine *motte and bailey castle* associated with the early
     Bishops of Hereford.

272  SO 294896  62 N.W.
     By the spot level 1151 used to stand the old *milestone*—'London 160'.

273  SO 259909  62 N.W.
     *Offa's Dyke* runs a few yards S. of the Baptist Chapel, and then the road S.
     runs along its flattened crest.

274  SO 247904  62 N.W.
     The *place-name* Cwm Lladron = the Robber's Valley.

275  SO 258900  62 N.W.
     At spot level 1106, *Offa's dyke* is damaged by cultivation.

276  SO 247895  62 N.W.
     The road here is the Kerry Hill *ridgeway* (Yr Hên Ffordd or London

Coachroad), following the R.D. Boundary. N.B. the bend of the boundary through an original Dyke gap. In the field N. of road and E. of Dyke is the site of Windy Hall.

277   SO 343904   62 N.E.
Just W. of the road and of the spot level 601 was found a *celt* in 1928.

278   SO 340892   62 N.E.
The Bishop's Castle *railway* ceased to function in 1935, when the track was demolished. Only the site of the track remains.

279   SO 326884   62 N.E.
*Old Hall* is also known as Blundell Old Hall, and an original coachroad *milestone* once stood here.

280   SO 336880 62 N.E.
Around Snakescroft a number of *flints* were found by Major Sykes of Lydham.

281   SO 298902   62 N.E.
In this field is a survival of *Celtic fields* and old lanes.

282   SO 299905   62 N.E.
Between the words 'Upper' and 'Beech' in a S.E. curve to the Borough Boundary is an unrecorded *earthwork*.

283   SO 295896   62 N.E.
The London *coachroad* from the W., swings S.E. at the fork. At the present bend before Caeglas the original went straight on across one field and along two field boundaries to join a footpath, down Kerry Green, past Bishop's Castle church, and straight on to Crowgate which is one of the coachroad toll houses.

284   SO 315888   62 N.E.
This *well* on the original track is known as 'the Christian's Well'.

285   SO 271851   62 S.W.
By the Guide Post (G.P. on map) is the site of a *pound*, the walling of which was extant in 1954.

286   SO 275847   62 S.W.
In this field, a light grey *flint scraper and flake* were found in 1957.

287   SO 265852   62 S.W.
Halfway down this field from the road and 100 ft. from the W. hedge is the *site* of Domlet *House* which had disappeared before 1836 (see Tithe Enclosure Award map of 1836).

288 SO 269851 62 S.W.
This is the site of the original Three Gates *farmhouse* which has disappeared since 1836.

289 SO 282846 62 S.W.
A brownish *flint scraper* was found here on 1st May 1954 by W. E. Lello.

290 SO 247862 62 S.W.
The 'Irish' *ridgeway* traverses S.E. to Offa's Dyke where it passes N.E. through an original pre-Offan gap in a curve along the footpath round the N. flank of the Hergan to join the present road at Three Gates (behind the house). Where it passes through the Dyke is a short portion of the boundary of Old Shadwell Township which finished at the Dyke.

291 SO 276868 62 S.W.
The air photograph shows an inturned entrance at the N. edge. It is more likely to be a herdsman's *defended dwelling*, and not military as suggested by the promontory fortress description in the Victoria County History of Shropshire.

292 SO 256862 62 S.W.
This *camp* is a forward earthwork to Offa's Dyke; it is a small *promontory fort* and is probably the village site of a pastoral group.

293 SO 257854 62 S.W.
On Skelton's Bank, when viewed from Maesyrhaem Hill, in the W., is a curious *circle* at this spot with radiating arms.

294 SO 259851 62 S.W.
This *tumulus* is correct, but damaged by implements, as reported to the Ancient Monuments Board.

295 SO 263854 62 S.W.
When seen from distant high ground, there appears to be something akin to a *disc barrow* between the 'H' and the 'e' of 'Hergan'.

296 SO 263874 62 S.W.
In the enclosure between the road and the brook W. of the ford, mediaeval pottery *sherds* have been found. S. of the ford, *Offa's Dyke* has been levelled.

297 SO 335846 62 S.E.
The so-called tumulus at Lower Down is a *motte*, just N. of which are earthworks adjoining and foundations which may possibly be a *Deserted Mediaeval Village*.

298 SO 341861 62 S.E.
On the 1886 O.S. map, this is part of a *road* which comes up by Springhead

at the S. edge of the map, past Lower Down, just W. of Walcot cottage, then due N. crossing the main road direct to the property on the lane S.W. of Mear's Barn, then N.W. direct to Stank Lane which is the London coachroad.

299   SO 338859   62 S.E.
These *fields* are reported to be *Celtic*.

300   SO 335860   62 S.E.
This *road* S. is the alternative road made by the great Lord Clive as compensation for his diversion of the original old road noted above in record no. 298. (see *Shrops. Arch. Soc. Trans.* vol. lv, 1954, p. 94 et seq). The old road too corresponds to what may be an old *Roman road* from the lead mines at Shelve in the N. to Leintwardine in S.

301   SO 310855   62 S.E.
S. of Pant Edward is a *mound* which is similar to the mound on the opposite Acton Bank (the latter is thought by some to be a promontory fortress rather than a tumulus).

302   SO 315851   62 S.E.
This appears to be correctly recorded as a *tumulus,* although some have suggested that it may be a small promontory fortress in spite of its being rather shallow.

303   SO 320871   62 S.E.
This not a tumulus, but a *motte*.

304   SO 339875   62 S.E.
This is the 'Conery *Field*' in which *flints* were found in 1921; all have been lost except one flint scraper.

305   SO 335873   62 S.E.
A *flint arrowhead* was found in this field in 1884.

306   SO 334870   62 S.E.
In each of the fields E. of Conery farm to Long Nursery and up to Stank Lane, *flint implements* have been found.

307   SO 386878   63 N.W.
An aerial photograph shows here *Celtic field systems* with a superimposed circular shallow mound. (*vide* report by O. G. S. Crawford in September 1954 issue of '*Antiquity*', following his visit and his interpretation to a field meeting in the spring of 1954). The small mounds on the site are *mediaeval 'pillows'*—artificial rabbit buries, and field systems of the Napoleonic War period are superimposed over part of the vast site. The circle is later and has obliterated the continuation of the field boundaries inside its perimeter.

308  SO 383876   63 N.W.

From N.E. to S.E. across the letter 'k' of Park Plantation is a hollow down which water runs. This may well be the end of the Portway which was a *mediaeval packhorse road* to Shrewsbury.

309  SO 374895   63 N.W.

This large round *tumulus* is thought by some to be Roman. Human bones were found in 1872 or earlier. The N.E. portion was cut into by road excavations. It rises from the supporting roadside wall.

310  SO 390895   63 N.W.

Just S.W. of Myndtown, a rectangular *enclosure* was reported by W. J. Hemp on 27th September 1937.

311  SO 388888   63 N.W.

Immediately inside the E. boundary of the spinney is a *healing well* which bubbles up through a hole in the centre of a stone trough, rectangular $3\frac{1}{2}$ ft. by $1\frac{1}{2}$ ft. The water is saline and the spring is as it was at least 70 years or more ago.

The stone just S. of the well is 6 ft. by 4 ft.—an angular recumbent *glacial erratic* of conglomerate rock; there is no evidence of its ever being upright or in any other position.

312  SO 354902   63 N.W.

This stone is a *glacial boulder*.

313  SO 366896   63 N.W.

Immediately N. of the road towards the S.E. end of the field is almost certainly a *round barrow*; though spread by cultivation, it is still about 6 ft. high and circular in an otherwise flat field. The S. edge of its perimeter is 7 yds. from the road and 44 yds. from the S.E. corner of the field (observed by Mrs. K. M. Bird).

314  SO 368906

This so-called tumulus is a *motte* (O.S. have since amended later editions). A large perforated basalt *axe-hammer* was found here, which is now in the Sir John Evans collection.

315  SO 370880   63 N.W.

The centre of Billing's Ring *hillfort* was ploughed in 1953.

316  SO 354899   63 N.W.

In the N.E. corner of the field in which Heath House stands is the site where a hoard of *Bronze spears* was found in 1862. The *field* is called 'The Bloody Romans'.

317   SO 344898   63 N.W.
>     This *road*, instead of bending N., originally went straight on to join the
>     footpath at the hedge on the E. side of the field due E. past 'The Bloody
>     Romans' (of record no. 316).

318   SO 348891   63 N.W.
>     This stone is a *glacial boulder*.

319   SO 437885   63 N.E.
>     The map shows the Watling Street *Roman road* taking the E. twisted road
>     instead of the straight footpath by the letter 'm' of 'Bushmoor' which is in
>     perfect alignment.

320   SO 399900   63 N.E.
>     The base of a probable *tumulus* may be located here.

321   SO 398900   63 N.E.
>     Huxter *stone* is a *natural* block according to Dr. Cobbold.

322   SO 408874   63 N.E.
>     This *road/track* to N.E. is thought by Col. Burne to have been the route
>     taken by Caratacus when he tried to reach Caer Caradoc at Church Stretton
>     to hold back the Romans from the other Caer Caradoc fort near Chapel
>     Lawn, S. of Clun, when the Romans were pressing down from the north.

323   SO 424901   63 N.E.
>     Between the ford and the footbridge on the N. bank of the stream is an old
>     *holy well* with *healing* properties for the cure of sore eyes.

324   SO 425904   63 N.E.
>     There are some double *terraces* between the 900ft. contour line and the
>     short path to the S.W. of the small spinney.

325   SO 385856   63 S.W.
>     'Stocks Well' is an old *stone well* about 4 ft. *square*, not circular, which may
>     be significant (? Roman).

326   SO 388844   63 S.W.
>     N. of Cabin and under the fork in the footpaths is an old yew tree and
>     *walling*, which may be significant.

327   SO 385871   63 S.W.
>     Just S. of Corn Mill and E. of the small footpath, there is an *earthwork* with
>     a ditch on the S. and E. only, and related to the homestead moat at the N.
>     and falling steeply W. to a damp hollow.

328   SQ 375866   63 S.W.
      The *place-name* Plowden = Ployden or Plovisdene of Saxon origin from
      Plean-dene (the Dane Hill).

329   SO 375873   63 S.W.
      The circle in the middle of the field is a *mound* on which trees are growing;
      it could be a barrow, but may be ornamental.

330   SO 364860   63 S.W.
      In the farmyard of the Redhouse is an original *cockpit* in good repair. It is
      stone built with thatched roof and of octagonal plan.

331   SO 343874   63 S.W.
      The London *coachroad* (here called Stank Lane) passes across the map to
      the E. edge at Basford. The 154 London *milestone* is original, as is also 157.
      The 156 London one is not shown on the map, but it exists at Bench Mark
      739·2 at grid 358867. 155 London is missing at B.M. on grid 371858.

332   SO 347875   63 S.W.
      In the S.W. corner of this field, a *flint blade* was found in 1935 by W.
      Morley Davies, (Miss Lily F. Chitty).

333   SO 350860   63 S.W.
      A *Roman bronze figurine* was found at Lydbury North in clay by the road-
      side. It is only about 6 ins. high of a helmeted, but otherwise naked,
      soldier carrying a towel draped over his arm. At the house called the 'Firs'
      near to the church there is a *moat*.

334   SO 402853   63 S.E.
      The writer regards the area around Upper Carwood as the *lost manor* of
      CAURTUNE in Domesday, because the place in 1393 is referred to in the
      name of Edgton which is called Eggedun—juxta-Caurwood.

335   SO 418849   63 S.E.
      Cheney Longville earthwork is a *motte and bailey castle*, as amended on the
      newer O.S. map editions.

336   SO 432870   63 S.E.
      Watling Street would appear to follow along the straight field boundaries
      which are in N. to S. alignment to the course of the *Roman road*, W. of the
      present deflection in the main road over Leamoor Common.

337   SO 402868   63 S.E.
      A *flint fabricator* was found in 1949 by the writer E. of the Castle Ring
      remains.

338   SO 391862   63 S.E.
        This *road* N.E. along the Ridgeway Hill and S. of Castle Ring is thought by
        Col. Burne to be Caratacus' route to Caer Caradoc at Church Stretton
        (see record no. 322).

339   SO 401848   63 S.E.
        The *hillfort* on Wart Hill is of irregular shape with two lines of scarps.

340   SO 412842   63 S.E.
        This is part of the London *coachroad* going N.W. to the W. edge of the map
        at Basford Bank. The *milestone* at Roundoak is missing, but the 152
        London is an original.

341   SO 191816   68 N.W.
        In the writer's opinion, the entire area around Llanllwyd needs careful
        study, both from the Deserted Mediaeval Village aspect in agricultural
        history, and also from the prehistoric aspect. From here have been collected
        a large quantity of *flints*, including some arrowheads of unusual design
        housed in Knighton Secondary Modern School, the collection of which
        was sponsored by Mr. Frank Noble among the school pupils. (see record
        345).

342   SO 194846   68 N.W.
        In this field, a *flint arrowhead* with 13 *artefacts* were found in 1954 by Mrs.
        Moody (of Anchor Inn) who passed them to me. Also a Bronze Age barbed
        and tanged *arrowhead* was found by Mrs. K. M. Bird in 1940.

343   SO 187818   68 N.W.
        A number of *flints* have been found in this field S. of the road by the
        writer.

344   SO 194816   68 N.W.
        On the N. margin of the road, a large *stone* lies in the ditch. Also in a line N.
        of this road in each field to either side of this stone are a few *tile quarries* of
        modern times.

345   SO 190815   68 N.W.
        The spinney W. of Llanllwyd is now felled. It is bounded on the N. by a
        wall of dressed stone continuing over the next three fields to the N.W.
        Inside the spinney area are some ground *depressions* comparing closely with
        those forming the cattle pound at Poundgate $\frac{3}{4}$ mile W.N.W. (see record
        341).

346   SO 178820   68 N.W.
        E. of the L-shaped spinney of old fir trees is an unrecorded *cattlepound*
        which was discovered (in conjunction with the late Mr. Tom Hamar of

Clun) by the late Mr. H. C. Jones, headmaster of Clungunford, in 1932 (*vide Trans. Caradoc & Severn Valley Field Club*, vol. ix, 1932-34, pp. 71-73). There is a clearly marked entrance to the S. at spot level 1201, which narrows to allow only one animal at a time to pass through to the first depression for branding and shoeing. He suggested that the other depressions up the W. side were personnel quarters, with stables at the N. for their horses. To the E. in adjoining fields are banked paddocks. The whole site unit would seem to represent one of the most eastern collecting points of cattle for the Drovers. In 1952, the late W. J. Slack believed it to be the common centre between the Clun and Kerry Lordships used for the Driving of the Common twice yearly. This was supported by John Lloyd of Rhydycwm who told his daughter that he remembered that stray cattle were driven here when the land was still common.

347   SO 170830   68 N.W.
> This is the area of the 17th C. *township* of Rhuganten, the original spelling of which appears to have been Rhiw-dan-tin.

348   SO 154835   68 N.W.
> The entrance to this *camp* is 12 ft. wide on the W. side; the circumference is 600 ft. and there are traces of a 6 ft. ditch.

349   SO 156822   68 N.W.
> Hendre stands on the site of an ancient *enclosure* (v. R.C.A.M. p. 22). Its corresponding 'Hafod' for seasonal transhumance activities is on the river Teme (v. 6″ O.S. Radnor sheet 4 N.E.)

350   SO 170816   68 N.W.
> The *ford* is now superseded by a bridge erected in 1950 (O.S. have amended).

351   SO 177818   68 N.W.
> This is a *quarry* which is not marked on the map.

352   SO 190818   68 N.W.
> S. of the road fork are unrecorded *earthworks and enclosures* which may have been connected with Welsh cattle trade activities.

353   SO 175840   68 N.W.
> Around this spot *flints* have been found when ploughed to 5 ins. deep.

354   SO 180837   68 N.W.
> *Flint implements* have been found here.

355   SO  184832   68 N.W.
      In the corner of this field by the 'G' of 'G.P.', a large grey leaf-shaped
      *arrowhead* of *flint* was found in 1955.

356   SO  167823   68 N.W.
      *Flint implements* have been found in this field E. of Vron Wood.

357   SO  164823   68 N.W.
      A little distance S.E. of Gorther, W. of the brook is a mound which may
      well be a *tumulus.*

358   SO  181823   68 N.W.
      The *mounds* here probably represent a disappeared building.  The next
      *field* to the E. and W. of the buildings (S. of the road) is called Rhygroes
      Piece.

359   SO  168843   68 N.W.
      During 1955, we obtained (author and family) 40 late Neolithic-Early
      Bronze Age *flint implements* and waste flakes from a circular site at 6 ins.
      deep and 20 yds. in diameter (specimens retained).

360   SO  171843   68 N.W.
      There was a *mound* here, but it was ploughed in February 1959.  No
      clear opinion as to whether it was natural or of archaeological interest.

361   SO  173841   68 N.W.
      Between May and July 1954 we obtained 219 *flint implements* and waste
      flakes from a circular area at 5 ins. deep and 8 yds. in diameter (specimens
      retained).  They appear to be late Neolithic to Early Bronze Age and
      suggest a chipping site.

362   SO  243821   68 NE.
      Possibly Newcastle derives its name from this 'new castle' *motte* (O.S. have
      since amended from tumulus) in the *field* called Craiggion.  A continuous
      low-lying area from the N. abrupt bend of the river passes to the N. and E.
      of the motte and rejoins the river to the S. in the same field.

363   SO  208836   68 N.E.
      Immediately W. of Hall of the Forest buildings on the N. of the road, is an
      earthwork *mound* known as 'the hospital' (cf. *hospitium* = Welsh yspyty).
      Hall of the Forest is reputed to be the site of the third hunting lodge out in
      Clun Forest used by the early Lords of Clun Castle.  The original house
      was built by the widow of Henry Fitz Alan in 1550 and is also known as
      'The Ladies' Hall'.  (see record no. 371).

364   SO  208816   68 N.E.
      Ladywell is a *holy well* with *healing* properties, associated with the early

history of the nearby Betws y crwyn church; this *place-name* means the 'chapel of the skins' possibly from remunerating itinerant clergy from Abbey Cwmhir with skins and/or wool for religious services in the parish.

365   SO  199822   68 N.E.
In the N.E. length of the wood are old *tile quarries*.

366   SO  205826   68 N.E.
Here is an ovate *earthwork*, which may be a quarry.

367   SO  197817   68 N.E.
This is a small length of the Springhill to Anchor *ridgeway*.

368   SO  203819   68 N.E.
Immediately E. of, and against Cow Hall farmhouse, is a possible mediaeval *enclosure*.

369   SO  239823   68 N.E.
At the S. end of the spinney are some *mounds* and hollows, which may be associated with Castle Idris fort.

370   SO  214818   68 N.E.
The *ford* W. of Moor Hall was bridged in 1950.

371   SO  216818   68 N.E.
Moor Hall was the second *hunting lodge* out from Clun Castle into the Clun Forest. The staircase is worthy of note, the newelpost is hollow to contain the spears, while the space beneath the flight of stairs has an iron grille in front, in which the hounds were temporarily penned during mealtimes. (see record no. 363).

372   SO  203822   68 N.E.
*Earthworks* here mark the site of a small earlier settlement.

373   SO  198845   68 N.E.
The curious *place-name* of Weal's Farm (or Weal's Old House) might just be from 'Wealh' = foreigner. This would be the view of a Welsh raider or settler from the English point of view. The name Wales appears to be of the same origin. Weal, however, is a common surname on the Border, and the farm could be so named.

374   SO  257846   68 N.E.
*Flint implements*, now in Clun Museum, have been found while ploughing this field.

375  SO 225835  68 N.E.
> *Flints* have been found on either side of the Ale Oak track road, and also in the next but one field, W. of the long spinney to the W. of the farmhouse.

376  SO 210819  68 N.E.
> Cwmiken is a typical Border stone house similar to a '*long house*', though it was ruinous in 1940.

377  SO 225822  68 N.E.
> Both *fords* at Upper Dyffryn were bridged in 1950 (O.S. since amended).

378  SO 194834  68 N.W.
> A grey *flint scraper* was found here in 1955.

379  SO 185835  68 N.W.
> The site of the 'Grey Stones *Stone Circle*' is now established. It is a little to the W. overlapping the map dotted line of the field ditch. Partial excavation in August 1955 confirmed a low composite stone wall, circular, but no burial was found at the centre. It was constructed prior to the formation of the hill peat. It appears to compare with the Pond Cairn barrow in Glamorgan, and if of the same period, it is the most northerly example so far revealed.

380  SO 182834  68 N.W.
> The old *name* for Mountflirt is Nant y pwllau = brook of the hollow. One spurious spelling is Pathley.

381  SO 188805 68 S.W.
> This is not a tumulus but a *motte and bailey castle,* as amended by O.S. on new map editions. It is of some importance in the Tempsiter ( = Temesider) Manor of the Hundred of Clun.

382  SO 170799  68 S.W.
> The older portion of the *lead mines* was worked by the *Romans*. Visited with a party on 27th March 1940.

383  SO 194797  68 S.W.
> In Beguildy church is preserved an ancient chest which appears to be an adaptation of an original *dug-out canoe*. Cf. another possible example in Hopesay church, W. of Craven Arms in Shropshire. Beguildy = Bugaildy = the house of the shepherd.   (see record no. 483).

384  SO 182788  68 S.W.
> The *field* S. of the B.M. 1015·6 is called Twmp y cwm, but there is no record of a mound.

385 SO 150806  68 S.W.

The *place-name* Killowent = Cil Owen (name of the brook) is a mis-spelling.

386 SO 151797  68 S.W.

At Cwm yr hob in 1959 were found six *flints,* one of which appears to be a microlith.

387 SO 151786  68 S.W.

*Flints* were found here in 1933.

388 SO 162807  68 S.W.

This *field* W. of the road is called Maes y garreg on the Tithe Schedule No. 172, but there is no evidence of a stone.

389 SO 169813  68 S.W.

Crugyn Tump is a *motte and bailey castle.*

390 SO 170812  68 S.W.

Somewhere in this area was a meadow called 'Bloody *Field*', where it was said that soldiers were buried after a battle; it cannot be identified today.

391 SO 204785  68 S.E.

At Bryndraenog, in the *field* next to the one called 'Devil's Kitchen', has been found a perforated picrite stone *axehead.* The gallery around the entrance hall of the house is dated 1636.

392 SO 240813  68 S.E.

The *place-name* Hongrass = Hên groes which probably refers to the cross-roads rather than to a cross; yet the disused cottage N.E. of the word 'Hongrass' on the edge of the map is known as Mount Abbey.

393 SO 215800  68 S.E.

Within a small radius of this spot, a number of *flint artefacts* have been found (Clun Museum).

394 SO 213795  68 S.E.

In the S.E. corner of this field, a *flint* implement was found.

395 SO 214797  68 S.E.

In the W. corner of this field, is a ploughed-down *mound* of black earth with a stoney centre.

396 SO 199794  68 S.E.

The circle in the paddock at Pantycaregl S. of the road is a *moated enclosure.*

397   SO  201791   68 S.E.
      In the *field* called maes y garreg, the *standing stone* is 5 ft. above ground and
      2 ft. wide.  It is prehistoric.

398   SO  210783   68 S.E.
      This is an undisturbed *tumulus*, probably Bronze Age, standing $5\frac{1}{2}$ ft. high
      and   280 ft. in circumference.

399   SO  274836   69 N.W.
      In the slang field (Lane House, Mardu) just N. of the Methodist Chapel is
      a pond to the E. of the sledge track.  On the edge of this pond (partly dried
      out in 1945) was found by Mrs. K. M. Bird a *Whitby jet bead* of the Offan
      Period;  this was confirmed on examination by Professor C. F. Hawkes to
      whom I took it when he was visiting Miss Lily F. Chitty.  (specimen
      retained).

400   SO  284815   69 N.W.
      Opposite the end of the drive on the N. side of the road at Oak Barn, once
      stood an old hollow *oak tree* in which was a Post Office *letter-box*.  The tree
      was later felled to widen the road;  it was known as the Post Office Oak.

401   SO  291818   69 N.W.
      This 'camp', amended to *earthwork*, is now thought by some to be a small
      *moraine*.  The writer supports this view, having recovered pieces of Upper
      Triassic sandstone bearing the fossil *Pecten valoniensis* in 1956 (*vide*
      Lyell's *Geology* p. 243).

402   SO  284825   69 N.W.
      The *mounds* here are not tumuli, but constitute the site of a disappeared
      *windmill.*

403   SO  289826   69 N.W.
      This is not a tumulus (amended to mound on later map editions).  It is
      simply an incomplete *earthwork.*

404   SO  274827   69 N.W.
      At the B.M. in the village centre, is the site of a *smithy.*

405   SO  276838   69 N.W.
      On the top of the ridge towards the S. corner of the field N. of the printed
      'e' of 'Cefns', was a possible *flint chipping site*;  when the field was ploughed
      in 1945, the writer found up to 50 flints concentrated in a clearly defined
      circle.

406   SO  277819   69 N.W.
      Opposite the guide-post, in the indentation of the S. margin of the road,

was a *cattle pound* on the 1836 Clun Enclosure map. Some masonry was visible in 1953.

407   SO 285820   69 N.W.

This spot marks a *mound* fairly similar to the one in the 'Oaks' field, E. of the ridgeway and S. of the road to Bicton.

408   SO 287820   69 N.W.

In the 'Oaks' field there formerly was a *mound* which on excavation proved to be a *burial* of possible Bronze Age date. (published by H. C. Jones; see Bibliography).

409   SO 288822   69 N.W.

A distinct *mound* 18 yds. in diameter and circular is just W. of the road. It is now spread out and shows darker coloured soil. The *field* is called Tumpy Moat.

410   SO 28382469 N.W.

The writer found a fine dark *flint scraper* in 1955 on the 800 ft. contour.

411   SO 276824   69 N.W.

This *menhir* (The Whitcott Stone) was standing until March 1944, when John Davies of Whitcott Hall pushed it over 'as being unsafe for his stock' to quote his words. It is almost certain to be a 'dolmen idol' being of the 'female' diamond shape (fertility culture), as well as signposting the ford over the river via a track down from the Springhill ridgeway to the S. across the valley to the 'Irish' trackway to the N. The *field* to the S. of the menhir, between the river and the main road to Clun, is called 'Dol Reaves' in which the sunken track to the ford and stone can be seen, especially when the sun is low to the W.

412   SO 278824   69 N.W.

In the field E. of the spot level 666 I found three *flints* in August 1955.

413   SO 254835   69 N.W.

In most of the fields W. of Cefn Bronydd *flint implements* have been found, as well as W. of the Rhespass and Bridge Farms to the N. (finders: the author's family, and the Fletcher family of Rhespass).

414   SO 266826   69 N.W.

This *field* S. of the road is known as Bryn Wicket (? corruption of Whitcott), with a *mound*, on which is an old oak tree. This appears to be the caput of a Celtic habitation site of the pre-Norman 'ceisydd'. If so, it explains the *village name* of Whitcott Keysett = the white cottage or dwelling of the ceisydd ( = the bailiff who collected the dues).

415   SO 256821   69 N.W.

The farmhouse of Lower Spoad is of immense interest on Offa's Dyke, being the first *hunting lodge* out from Clun Castle into the Clun Forest. It contains an excellent piece of mediaeval carving on the face of a solid oak beam over the open chimney, which represents a hunting scene with boar-hounds (the six with collars), staghounds with stag and hind (the latter transfixed with a large arrow); the stricken hind is quite reminiscent of the Lasceaux cave paintings.

Southwards from the farmyard, *Offa's Dyke* has a scarp of 24 ft. to the crest.

416   SO 251825   69 N.W.

A little W. of the school and on the S. side of the road, is the site of a *pound* on the 1836 Clun Enclosure map.

417   SO 256834   69 N.W.

The line of *Offa's Dyke* N. from this point for 400 yds. should be shown as being more massive, being built up from the spoil holes on the upper E. slope. Here also is an original gap for drainage.

418   SO 250827   69 N.W.

The original entrance to this *camp* is on the edge of the steep slope in the S.W. corner.

419   SO 256825   69 N.W.

S. of Bryndreinog, a section of *Offa's Dyke* appears at the water's edge on the N. bank of the river Clun; but S. of the river, the Clun itself is used as part of the Dyke alignment N. to S. From spot level 663 the Dyke becomes more pronounced along the alluvial flats to the road at the Lower Spoad.

420   SO 261843   69 N.W.

The stream from N. of the Mount farm runs down the ditch of *Offa's Dyke* and has eroded it deeply. The Dyke, by its construction, deflected its course, but the original pre-Offan course is still visible. Note here also the remains of two *cottages* with *beaten earth floors*.

421   SO 264843   69 N.W.

The building on which the B.M. is printed was a *wheelwright's* shop in 1936.

422   SO 268838   69 N.W.

There are three uninhabited *cottages* with *beaten earth floors*, and at least three others S. down the Mardu Lane between Lane House and Whitcott Keysett.

423   SO 283841   69 N.W.

The *place-name* Llanhedrick should be spelt Llanedric (associated with the legends of Wild Edric). Notice that 'Llan' = original Welsh for enclosure, there being no church.

424    SO 336942    69 N.E.
    There is a mound here which appears to be a *tumulus*.

425    SO 326837    69 N.E.
    In 1940 a Forestry Commission warden informed me that when (some 20 years earlier) they were digging on and around the camp ramparts at Bury Ditches, preparatory to planting conifers, a number of *flint axe-heads* (his description left no doubt) were found, and not knowing their significance, the men re-buried them there. He could not remember the spot or vicinity.

426    SO 335817    69 N.E.
    The *placename* Gunridge is probably a corruption of Gunward, the Saxon landowner *tempore regis Edwardi* mentioned in Domesday under Clungunford, which was Gunward's portion of the Clun estates which he held under Picot de Say.

427    SO 300818    69 N.E.
    The *mounds* around here represent the site of mediaeval criminal executions; the *field* is known as '*Gallows*tree Meadow'.

428    SO 299812    69 N.E.
    The present Villa Farmhouse is only a portion of the original (probable) *Priest's house.* There are Norman windows blocked up on the N. side, and the mound to the W. adjacent would appear to represent the ruins of the main building block.

429    SO 321828    69 N.E.
    Arc-shaped *earthworks* (under the word 'knoll') are probably the site of an outpost to the Bury Ditches hill-fort to the N.

430    SO 330835    69 N.E.
    The *placename* Sunnyhill is called Tangley Hill in Auden's '*Little Guide to Shropshire*'.

431    SO 300836    69 N.E.
    The original main *road* from Clun to Bishop's Castle forked N.E. at the B.M. 867·1, past the small building through Colstey Farm to Acton further N.

432    SO 304841    69 N.E.
    The B.M. 805·4 is at the roadside end of a boundary between two fields, W. of the road. In the E. corner of the southernmost there appears to be a much-spread *mound*, while the northern *field* is called 'Castle Field'.

433    SO 297833    69 N.E.
    Harp House is quite commonly associated with the *Welsh Drovers* (and hence the Welsh harp).

434 SO 302818   69 N.E.
>A *stone* is marked here on the 1836 Clun Enclosure Award map.

435 SO 275803   69 S.W.
>Both here and also at 274802 & 273804, on the terrace above the ridge, the writer and family in 1954 found a concentration of over 200 *flint flakes and implements*. The siting of these surface finds, after ploughing and cultivation, suggest that at least three settlement spots exist, but there may well be more. They are of Neolithic type and of dark patination (specimens retained). The three suggested sites stretch S.E. from the printed figure 8 of the B.M. 1200·8, approximately 300 ft. N. of, and parallel to, the Spring-hill ridgeway.

436 SO 256803   69 S.W.
>A *flint arrowhead* was found in this field.

437 SO 254800   69 S.W.
>A large stone in this field is possibly a *hoarstone*.

438 SO 281781   69 S.W.
>The *placename* Treverward was first recorded as Burwardston (i.e. first settled by Saxons); then it changed to Tref Burward showing that the Welsh took over from the Saxons.

439 SO 284804   69 S.W.
>S. from the point where the 1000 ft. contour crosses the road, a slight *hollow-way* is visible along the hedge S.W. in line with the 'Heartstone' (see record no. 456).

440 SO 281794   69 S.W.
>Between the 'i' and the 'l' of 'Hill', is a possible *tumulus*.

441 SO 268808   69 S.W.
>A *flint flake* has been found at the E. end of the field.

442 SO 269803   69 S.W.
>Three *flint implements* and 7 chipped flint nodules were found here in July 1962 by Basil Lello (of no. 1 Mardu) while draining the land at 18 ins. deep; also a stone *hand celt* 148mm × 50mm × 30mm.

443 SO 272805   69 S.W.
>The writer has found a number of *flints* above the old quarry.

444 SO 276807   69 S.W.
>A leaf-shaped *arrowhead* (18mm × 33mm) was found by Basil Lello just E. of the 1000 ft. contour, and another at the S. end of the field.

445 SO 277806   69 S.W.
> B. Lello found a *flint* just E. of the spinney.

446 SO 279807   69 S.W.
> Three *flints* were found by B. Lello at the top of the field.

447 SO 279804   69 S.W.
> A *flint* was found by B. Lello between the two footpaths.

448 SO 283807   69 S.W.
> A *flint* and 2 chert implements were found by B. Lello between the building and the S. end of the wood.

449 SO 279812   69 S.W.
> Three *flint* flakes were found by B. Lello in 1962.

450 SO 277802   69 S.W.
> A *flint* was found by B. Lello on the S. edge of the footpath.

451 SO 290793   69 S.W.
> Immediately E. of the road is an unrecorded *megalith*.

452 SO 292793   69 S.W.
> There is another recumbent *megalith* here.

453 SO 291792   69 S.W.
> In the boundary hedge is another recumbent *megalith*.

454 SO 292787   69 S.W.
> The *field* N. of the printed spot level 1195 is called 'Camp Field', where the late George Luff collected a great number of *flints* in his pioneer antiquarian research in the Clun area when headmaster of Clun school.

455 SO 284783   69 S.W.
> On the E. side of the road (340 ft. N.W. of Foest), lying on its side over the ditch, is a stone $4\frac{1}{2}$ ft. by 3 ft. by 2 ft. It may be a *hoarstone*, though it could have archaeological associations, perhaps having been moved from its original position.

456 SO 278796   69 S.W.
> At 900 ft. from the spring, due S. on a line drawn from the spring to the base of the letter 'R' of 'Rock', is a recumbent *menhir* known as the 'Heartstone'. It is 8 ft. by 7 ft. by $2\frac{1}{2}$ ft. and is the broad 'female' type. It is considered that this stone is the most important menhir in the area. It seems to be the directional focal point locally in that it lies at the intersection of ancient trackways :—

(a) N.E. via Weston to the Whitcott stone on the river Clun (record 411).

(b) S.E. to 'Camp Field' flint site and Penywern stone circle (record 453).

(c) N.W. to join the Springhill ridgeway through to the Kerry Hill stone circle.

457   SO 265805   69 S.W.

This open ground was Burfield Warren; it was enclosed before the Enclosure Act of 1839, and also used for common grazing. There was a considerable settlement around the church site prior to 1839, and it is thus classed as a *decayed township*; only the one farm now remains (see records nos. 462 and 466).

458   SO 264795   69 S.W.

From the point of the parish boundary fence E. to the 100 ft. contour within this enclosure is a *track* which is called Clwydd Melin (? site of mill), at the E. end of which is a *circle* called Garnedd David. The stream S.W. is called Cwm Cae Madoc Gutter.

459   SO 267798   69 S.W.

The second *field* E. of Burfield is called Hoar Stone.

460   SO 250796   69 S.W.

At 360 ft. S.W. of the spot level 1268, and 560 ft. N.W. of the spot level 1306, is a possible *tumulus* 39 ft. in diameter and 62 yds. in circumference. Also 300 ft. on the same line N.W. from spot level 1306 is a very large oval mound which appears to be man-made and is possibly Offan.

461   SO 265780   69 S.W.

This little enclosure is straight-sided with rounded corners, and in a slight hollow. It is sited for protection, not against man, but against the weather. It was probably a *cattle enclosure*, the entrance to which is not clearly defined.

462   SO 263801   69 S.W.

At Burfield (formerly Warren House) in 1957 there was found a large copper-bronze *Roman coin* (c. 170 A.D.); it is now in Clun Museum. (see records no. 457 & 465).

463   SO 255808   69 S.W.

*Offa's Dyke* was here broken to allow the Springhill ridgeway to pass through; the gap is therefore original. The *ridgeway* reaches here from the W. edge of the map, at first E., then S.E. over the Burfield crossroads, over Rockhill and on to Clun Hill on the E. edge of the map.

464 SO 256784 69 S.W.
> The highest point reached by *Offa's Dyke* over its entire length is at the spot level 1408 on Llanvair Hill.

465 SO 251798 69 S.W.
> The hollow immediately E. of the fork in the road is a possible outpost to *Offa's Dyke*.

466 SO 260802 69 S.W.
> The large oval mound in the field E. of the spinney is the *site* of Burfield *church* destroyed in 1401 A.D. by Owain Glyndŵr.

467 SO 292788 69 S.E.
> On the S. grassy roadside verge of the ridgeway, for 1100 ft. from the W. edge of the map, are several fragments of a destroyed *monolith* which was extant in situ in the 19th C.

468 SO 314788 69 S.E.
> In the S.W. corner of the field, N. of that in which the word 'Hill' is printed, is a now recumbent *megalith*; it was partly upright in 1904. It is 10 ft. long, 4 ft. wide and 4 ft. thick. It was originally 4 ft. in the ground.

469 SO 330781 69 S.E.
> N.W. of Newhouse to Fiddler's Elbow is an old *trackway*.

470 SO 320787 69 S.E.
> On the N. side of the quarry track is a recumbent *megalith* in the heather.

471 SO 297790 69 S.E.
> This is the site of the largest *megalith* in the area—14ft. long, 4 ft. wide and 2 ft. thick. It was buried 3 ft. deep about 1865 A.D., and in a dry season it may be located as a cropmark.

472 SO 297788 69 S.E.
> Under the printed 'u' of 'Clun', on the N. verge of the road, lies a large stone which itself may be part of a removed *monolith*.

473 SO 293784 69 S.E.
> At the N.E. end of the second field S. of the ridgeway (on the edge of the map), is a recumbent *menhir* in the centre of a hollow. Miss Lily F. Chitty seemed to recognise a 'cup-mark' when we visited it.

474 SO 297809 69 S.E.
> Between the road and the 600 ft. contour, was dug out a circular ring of *masonry*, possibly connected with the Castle.

475 SO 301809 69 S.E.
>    S. of Newport Street and N. of High Street, the foundations of the vanished
>    *church* of St. Thomas are, in sections, visible in adjoining gardens around
>    the site.

476 SO 301806 69 S.E.
>    The Six Bells Inn, now a ruin, was formerly a *coaching inn*, but has been
>    destroyed by fire, and subsequently omitted from new map editions.

477 SO 297808 69 S.E.
>    This *field* is called Welshman's Leasow.

478 SO 292788 69 S.E.
>    The Springhill *ridgeway* crosses the map from the E.S.E. to the E. edge of
>    the map; the first field on the N. being part of the Camp Field (see record
>    no. 454).

479 SO 377830 70 N.W.
>    On the Beeches Hollow 'platform', *flints and sherds* of pottery have been
>    found.

480 SO 353816 70 N.W.
>    In 1928, *flints* were found in this field, also in the adjoining one to the E.
>    and in the one to the S.

481 SO 364822 70 N.W.
>    In the field N. of the spot level 566 was found a notched *arrowhead*.

482 SO 369815 70 N.W.
>    The *guide-post* is very old and made of stone.

483 SO 389833 70 N.W.
>    In Hopesay church is a possible *dug-out canoe* adapted as a church chest.
>    Cf. the similar example in Beguildy church in Radnorshire (see record
>    no. 383).

484 SO 380830 70 N.W.
>    A small, but fine, grey leaf-shaped *arrowhead* and 4 *flint scrapers* were
>    handed in to Clun Museum in August 1955, picked up on agricultural land
>    near to Burrow Hill fort.

485 SO 342843 70 N.W.
>    What is thought to be a *Roman track* from Leintwardine to the Roman lead
>    mines at Shelve should be plotted as follows: from the top of the W.
>    margin of the map in a S.E. direction, through the second 'o' of 800, then
>    through the capital 'C' of Walcot, along the track bordering the S. margin
>    of Park Plantation, N.E. of Sheepcote Quarry to the B.M. 505·8 at the W.

point of Kempton village, continuing on the W. side of the river Kemp due S. to the bottom of the sheet (see record no. 300). The map referred to is the 6″ County Series Shropshire LXX N.W.

486   SO 347817   70 N.W.
A *flint borer* was found in this field.

487   SO 350823   70 N.W.
This is the site of a *flint chipping-floor*; specimens from this Clunbury collection were in Clun Museum in 1958.

488   SO 432832   70 N.E.
Between the railway and the spot level 399 on the main road, a *Romano-British pot* (culinary, about 175 A.D.) was found when the mills of the South Shropshire Farmers' Ltd. were being built. Details are recorded by Miss Lily F. Chitty. I acquired the pot in 1953 from the sister of the finder (Mr. Owen of Aston-on-Clun). The Watling Street crosses the map from N. to S. only 600 yds. W. of the site. There is a very similar specimen in the Museum at Rowley's Mansion in Shrewsbury.

489   SO 396840   70 N.E.
The occupier of the house named 'The Fish' has a *Roman coin* (Nerva) which was found locally around Hopesay.

490   SO 412832   70 N.E.
At Sibdon Castle, a large collection of mediaeval *slipware* has been found.

491   SO 413842   70 N.E.
The 'Long Lane' which enters the N. edge of the map and goes to the N. of Newington and across the ford at Halford is the London *coachroad*. The *milestone* at B.M. 420·1 (SO 425837) is the original London 151. The road then aims for Quatford (nr. Bridgnorth) in E. Salop.
At Newington there was a *coaching inn* called the 'New Inn'.

492   SO 357809   70 S.W.
A mound in this field W. of the wood closely resembles a *tumulus*. It could be the 'laew' ( = Anglo-Saxon 'mound') of Purslow.

493   SO 372789   70 S.W.
*Three Ashes* is so-called from the 3 ash trees planted on the fork of the road at the guidepost, one in each of the parishes of Clunbury, Hopton Castle and Clungunford. The last one was not very vigorous in 1953, being only just alive.

494   SO 361805   70 S.W.
Somewhere about Purslow Bridge on the Clun river is thought to be '*amnis*

*vado incerto'* (Taciti Annalium Liber XII, 33 et seq) in recording the defeat of Caratacus. Supporters of this view suggest that after the river spate subsided, which they assume was occurring at the time, the Romans crossed *'haud difficulter'*, and engaged the Britons on the ridge of Purslow Wood and Clunbury Hill.

495    SO 340784   70 S.W.
> E. from B.M. 975·5 is Butterfield Lane for some 800 yds. to the B.M. 877·8, along which are 14 large *stones*. Their origin is yet unknown, but they appear to derive from *glacial erratics* which may have been blown up and removed from adjacent fields. They are all in the roadside ditches (12 on the S. side, and 2 on the N. side).

496    SO 358803   70 S.W.
> This footpath is thought by Lt. Col. Burne (*Shrops. Arch. Soc. Trans.* 1963 Pt. 1 pp. 40-41) to be part of the old *British track* from Caer Caradoc (at Church Stretton) to Caer Caradoc (at Chapel Lawn), and used by the Romans in the pursuit and defeat of Caratacus.

497    SO 375779   70 S.W.
> Half of the upper, and half of the lower stones of a *quern* were found here.

498    SO 352793   70 S.W.
> The Llan provides some important clues to archaeological research as follows :—
> (a)   it is possibly a *deserted* site of a *mediaeval village*; the field immediately N. of the house formerly contained some very old yews, felled about 1950.
> (b)   there are 2 stones N. of the house and near to it, but these are Rhayader grit *glacial* erratics.
> (c)   In the second field N. are some *earthworks*; subject to excavation, they could be the remains of a church.
> (d)   Up to 1954, Mr. J. Morgan (the owner/occupier) had ploughed 19 fields which had yielded over 400 *flints*, mostly of Wiltshire origin, though a few were Irish; possibly indicating bartering along the ridgeway; they are in Clun Museum. It should be noted how thickly clustered were the flint finds around the pools and the well.
> (e)   Several *cattle shoes* (cues) were also found.

499 SO 341798   70 S.W.
> The Springhill *ridgeway* (i.e. from Anchor to Onibury) runs from W. to E. via Three Ashes to the foot path at 389788.

500    SO 364784   70 S.W.
> The field N. of the church at Hopton Castle, and the next two E., formed one of the *Saxon common fields*.

501 SO 427783  70 S.E.
> *Flints* have been found in this field and the one adjoining E. at 430784.

502 SO 420800  70 S.E.
> It is reported that on the summit of View Edge (or Weo or Yeo Edge) are some *earthworks*.

503 SO 407783  70 S.E.
> Between Swanhill Coppice on Saddle Hill on the E. and the Watling Street on the W., S. from B.M. 562·46 for 1000 ft., is the site of a mediaeval *strip field system* of 15 strips.

504 SO 413802  70 S.E.
> The track of the *Roman Watling Street* is visible as a crop-mark S. of Weo Farm in a straight line S. (to the lane E. of Goat Hill) for 700 yds. The deflection of the present road is thus later.

505 SO 418788  70 S.E.
> *Flints* were found in this field in 1931.

506 SO 437784  70 S.E.
> Green Lane from the E. edge of the map is the Springhill *ridgeway* (Onibury to Anchor) going W. to Brandhill, Crossways, N. of Clungunford and Abcott.

507 SO 395788  70 S.E.
> This is not a tumulus, but a *motte*; it has been partly plundered and pottery was once found. It has been amended as such on new map editions.

508 SO 394787  70 S.E.
> E. of the church porch and S. of the church is the base of four steps of a *churchyard cross*.

509 SO 393786  70 S.E.
> The Rocke Arms is now only a *farm*, being formerly an inn.

510 SO 398777  70 S.E.
> In the field W. of the road B4367 and overlapping the three fields on the E. are 3 *lynchets*, which may be pre-Roman. They run from N.W. to S.E.

511 SO 404782  70 S.E.
> From N. to S. down the centre of the field S. of Crosshorn is another probable *lynchet*.

512 SO 464830  71 N.W.
> This *road* is locally called Castle Road, coming from Stokesay Castle.

513   SO 460816   71 N.W.
    On the E. side of the road (between the printed words 'Norton' and 'Old Quarry') in Crowther's Orchard, is the *site* of the *burial* of the dead from the battle of Stokesay on 19th June 1645. A number of human skeletons were dug up by workmen digging foundations for farm buildings. Local opinion is wrong in calling it a Roman cemetery.

514   SO 222770   75 N.E.
    This *tumulus* is 5 ft. high, 75 ft. in diameter and 240 ft. in circumference.

515   SO 228767   75 N.E.
    This *tumulus* was destroyed prior to October 1910.

516   SO 232771   75 N.E.
    Between the two paths immediately W. of the B.M. 792·7 is an unrecorded *mound*.

517   SO 240774   75 N.E.
    There is a *place-name* in old records N. of Llanvair Waterdine called Menethesney (cf. Mynydd = mountain), which could reasonably be Mount Pleasant.

518   SO 241763   75 N.E.
    Immediately opposite the inn on the N. side of the road, used to stand a *tithe barn*; it was demolished in 1951 for a car park! This road N.W. to Runnis is the old road from Knighton to Velindre along the N. bank of the river.

519   SO 197781   75 N.E.
    Just above the 1000 ft. contour W. of the wood is the site where a socketed *picrite axe hammer* was found.

520   SO 214760   75 N.E.
    A *spindle-whorl* was found here.

521   SO 220758   75 N.E.
    This *field* is called 'Castle Bedwt', but it has no known significance.

522   SO 215780   75 N.E.
    The area around Red Wood is Crewilsey, referred to in the *Hearth Tax Roll*.

523   SO 224775   75 N.E.
    This area S.E. of Llanwolley is Ffynnon Fair, referred to in the *Hearth Tax Roll*. (see W. J. Slack in Bibliography).

524   SO 269760   76 N.W.

      The gap in *Offa's Dyke* N. of this point to Brynorgan is marked on the 1833 O.S. 1″ map as a dotted line. It has been quarried away for a few yards S. of Brynorgan.

525   SO 270755   76 N.W.

      The *Dyke* has an E. ditch from here to the corner southwards. This triangular corner may be a post-Offan modification for use when the beacon was lit on the hilltop.

526   SO 274749   76 N.W.

      Just W. of *Offa's Dyke* and N. of the track is the site where *flints* were discovered by W. A. Cummins of Skyborry. The Dyke material was at this point taken from the E. side as the darker grass shows.

527   SO 283754   76 N.W.

      At the S. end of the narrow spinney in the right angle of footpaths S. of the R.D.Bdy, is the site of a *vanished church* and burial ground, to the E. of which is an old *milestone*. The boundary brook is known as Gore Gutter. In Eyton's *Antiquities* it is mentioned that in the Inquisition of 1272 and 1291 there was a township of Llangornes in this district, but so far not identified. Within living memory, the church site was referred to as 'Old Stow Church', and there is a bridle road across to the Church Field at Stow. It thus seems likely that this is the site of the *deserted mediaeval village* of GOREHAM.

528   SO 284771   76 N.W.

      A picrite *hammerstone* was handed in to Clun Museum in 1956. It was found built into the wall of this house in the hamlet of Purlogue.

529   SO 284769   76 N.W.

      On the S. edge of the lane is the site of a *pound*. The two *fields* between the bend of the brook and the Liney Lane (i.e. across the lane opposite the house in record no. 528) are jointly called 'Pound Close'.

530   SO 291757   76 N.W.

      About 70 yds. N. of the spot level 1035 is the site where a *stone axe* was discovered by Michael Gray in 1950.

531   SO 270756   76 N.W.

      The *place-name* Sanaham = the old name Sannwm.

532   SO 260777   76 N.W.

      The scarp of *Offa's Dyke* is here 29 ft.

533   SO 261775   76 N.W.

      There is a 10 ft. wide drainage gap in *Offa's Dyke* here, S. of which the ground is boggy.

534   SO 266767   76 N.W.
      There are spoil holes E. of *Offa's Dyke*.

535   SO 269768   76 N.W.
      E. from the spot level 978, but S. of the Drowsey Lane, curving round to
      Drowsey farm is a well-defined *hollow-way*.

536   SO 279779   76 N.W.
      In the middle of the field, between the angle of the two field-lanes, is what
      appears to be a *mound*, with an oak tree on it.

537   SO 284772   76 N.W.
      There is a large *stone* in the brook; the adjacent field is called 'Stone
      Close'.

538   SO 320749   76 N.E.
      This *spring* is called 'Pistyll well' on the 1842 Stow Boundary map.

539   SO 324752   76 N.E.
      A *spindle-whorl* was found here in 1954, and another in the same field
      immediately N. Both are in Knighton Secondary School (per Frank Noble)

540   SO 310771   76 N.E.
      The *place-name* 'Wheelbarrow' is likely to have been derived from 'weala'
      ( = Welshman). The *field* at the N.W. end is called the 'Harp Piece'.

541   SO 311767   76 N.E.
      This track is a *hollow-way*.

542   SO 319779   76 N.E.
      In the S.E. fork of these cross-tracks is a *hoarstone*.

543   SO 315766   76 N.E.
      The N. to S. boundary banks throughout the length of Brineddin Wood are
      mediaeval *quillets*, or portions of the wooded area allocated for the rights of
      pannage ( = the foraging of acorns by pigs).

544   SO 336774   76 N.E.
      At the righthand side of the spring is the spot where a polished grey *flint
      celt* was found by the footpath by A. V. Bedwell, a worker from Hagley
      Farm in January 1954 and deposited in Clun Museum.

545   SO 297747   76 N.E.
      This footpath N. to the R.D.C. Bdy. and along the hedge N.E. to the
      spinney, then N. to the stream and N.W. along the stream towards the
      Black Garn, is a *lost track* to the Garn and to Bryncambric, being a bridle
      road from Knighton.

546   SO 300753   76 N.E.

> This point is the centre of an *earthwork* with single ditch and bank 4 ft. at the maximum at the N.E.

547   SO 297749   76 N.E.

> At the crossing of the two tracks where the R.D.C. Bdy. joins it, is a '*suicide's grave*'. The Boundary agreement between Stow and Clun in 1843 marks it on the map as 'Russin's Grave', whereas on the Lurkenhope Commons Enclosure Map of 1850 (1854 award) it is marked as 'Russell's Grave'.

548   SO 302764   76 N.E.

> Between the figures 800 and 900 this *placename* is 'Hongar Hill' which possibly = hên gaer (the old camp); S.E. of this to the W. of the bend in the road is a *hollow-way*.

549   SO 306761   76 N.E.

> A grey *flint scraper* was found on a rabbit bury on 1st June 1954 by Mrs. L. C. Lloyd of Shrewsbury (who retained it). Reported at a field meeting of the Shrops. Arch. Soc.

550   SO 310759   76 N.E.

> Within the N. fortifications, the vegetation suggests a possible site of a *well or spring*.

551   SO 296751   76 N.E.

> A Mesolithic or Neolithic 'B' *flint pick*, and also an *arrowhead*, were found here by Michael Gray; the former is in Shrewsbury Museum, and the latter at the Comprehensive Secondary School at Knighton.

552   SO 290723   76 S.W.

> Bryn y Castell is a fine *motte* 500 ft. in circumference, 20 ft. high and its flat summit is 50 ft. in diameter; the ditch is 15ft. wide. If ever a bailey existed, it would have been to the S. and obliterated by cultivation.

553   SO 283730   76 S.W.

> The *place-name* Panpunton = pen pwnton meaning the head of the waters where they were dammed up to supply the mills (see weir and mills lower down the stream). This explanation is more likely than any reference to flooding by the river Teme. Note also that 'pwn' is a sack of corn, and that 'pynfarch' = mill-race.

554   SO 278718   76 S.W.

> Jackets Well is a *healing well* for internal or external use for sprains and rheumatism. It was formerly known as St. Edward's Well, and was thus a *holy well* also. The name 'Jacket' is possibly the Welsh word iachâd = healing, though this is by no means certain.

555   SO 277717   76 S.W.

Just S. of Jackets Well (record no. 554) in 1935, the road was widened and a *barrow* came to light (not hitherto recorded), when it was cut through. It contained a Middle Bronze Age cinerary urn, found under a stone cairn capped with earth, as well as the rim of another one; it is in the National Museum of Wales, Cardiff.

556   SO 279744   76 S.W.

S. from above the 'D' of 'Dike' for 900 ft., the E. ditch of *Offa's Dyke* is ploughed in, and there is no W. ditch. S. again to the 'u' of Panpunton (700 ft.), the Dyke often passes a rock outcrop and the E. ditch cuts into the rock 2 to 3 ft. deep. Then for 1300 ft. the E. ditch is merely a succession of spoil holes proving that the Dyke was the boundary bank. Beyond this point, field evidence is absent S. to the river Teme, but the missing portion is likely to have followed the present parish boundary.

557   SO 284723   76 S.W.

Knighton Castle is a flat-topped *motte* 50 ft. in diameter, with traces of a moat. A 17th C. wall was built round it. It was destroyed in 1262 by Llewellyn ap Gruffydd.

558   SO 250745   76 S.W.

Near Cnwclas Castle is a *field* called 'The Bloody Field'. There is also reputed to be a *tumulus* on the site of the battle of 1146; this was opened in the 19th C. and found to be 5-chambered. Furthermore, Jonathan Williams in his '*Radnorshire*' refers to a barrow opened about 1790 containing bones and urns.

559   SO 256743   76 S.W.

It is thought that one or other of the two *fields* S. of the Teme and S.E. of Lower House Farm may be 'The Bloody Field' (of record no. 558).

560   SO 264745   76 S.W.

The *place-name* Skyborry = the Welsh ysguboriau = barns.

561   SO 270740   76 S.W.

In the N.W. angle of the grid lines at this point is an unrecorded *barrow*. The river has changed its course appreciably.

562   SO 250745   76 S.W.

Apart from the motte and bailey baronial stronghold which was held by the Mortimers until the reign of Henry VI, there was probably an earlier *hillfort*. It is suggested that it was once known as Caer Gogyrfen, as 'Kayrogheren' is named among certain Radnor estates belonging to Abbey Cwmhir. It was laid waste by Owain Glyndŵr as recorded in the Patent Roll of 1406. Kayrogheren is, however, comparable to Carreg y fran ( =the rock of the crow), 1 mile S.W. of Bugeildy on the Warren Brook.

563   SO 263738   76 S.W.

Edward Lhuyd in *'Parochialia' ii*, 38 calls the *place-name* Craig y don (1698). Craig Donn was "where they formerly dug for money". It is a natural outcrop of rock.

564   SO 259731   76 S.W.

The *place-name* White Anthony is called Weidanleu by Edward Lhuyd; it also appears to have once been called Llandillo.

565   SO 264735   76 S.W.

In 1958-59, approximately 30 pieces of *flint* were found around Craigydon farm, among which was a leaf-shaped arrowhead, and another broken one.

566   SO 243742   76 S.W.

A *beam* at Pentrusco is dated 1678, but the house is fairly modern.

567   SO 274745   76 S.W.

A *hammer-stone* was found here by W. Cummins of Skyborry.

568   SO 274744   76 S.W.

13th and 14th C. *pottery* has been found here by W. Cummins.

569   SO 275744   76 S.W.

*Flints* were found here by W. Cummins in 1953.

570   SO 322734   76 S.E.

Between the E. edge of Tornett wood and the spot level 765 is, from ground observations, probably the site of the *Deserted Mediaeval Village* of Thornton of the Domesday Survey.

571   SO 330730   76 S.E.

This *motte and bailey* (as amended on new map editions) is the original 'Stanage Castle' which on older O.S. maps was wrongly marked and later correctly deleted from the Park at 334716.

572   SO 309736   76 S.E.

In the Vicarage garden (i.e. between the house and the printed word 'Vicarage') were found two portions of an 11*th* C. *seal*; they have so far not been identified by the National Museum of Wales at Cardiff.

573   SO 313727   76 S.E.

*Cattle shoes* have been dug up at Milebrook. Rev. J. C. Williams of Letton, Hereford, has heard of a large heap of cattle shoes being dug up at Norton (near Knighton), and believes they went to Presteigne.

574   SO 315717   76 S.E.

For the *place-name* Cwm Copa, *vide* George Borrow's "*Lavengro*" for the word 'coper' meaning a 'horse-dealer'. Associated with the cattle shoes above (in record no. 573), it could provide a link with the Welsh Drovers.

575  SO 305745  76 S.E.
There are reports (from Mr. Foster of Knighton, forestry worker) that a number of *flint* finds and (?) pottery have been found on Stow Hill.

576  SO 299742  76 S.E.
Halfway along the E. edge of the footpath was found a polished *flint axehead* by the Sexton of Stow, James Morgan, about 1934, who loaned it to Shrewsbury Museum in 1954.

577  SO 308740  76 S.E.
Between the two footpaths is a possible unrecorded *motte*.

578  SO 310736  76 S.E.
E. of the vicarage, S. of the church and N. of the field drive are the *foundations* of a building; excavation yielded stratified pottery of the 15th-16th C.

579  SO 310734  76 S.E.
The *Roman villa* was partially dug in 1925 (records are with Rev. J. C. Williams, Letton, Hereford). It is quite likely to have been the residence of a Romanised Brython.

580  SO 312729  76 S.E.
In the corner N. of the wood, is an unrecorded low *tumulus*.

581  SO 310720  76 S.E.
Regarding the *place-name* 'Pitts' around this point, in a document of 1341 A.D. by the Assessors of the 9th Taxation, this site is referred to as Putteskenoule.

582  SO 307737  76 S.E.
This three angled *field* is called Edow ysgarvon, in which are remains of possible *Celtic fields*.

583  SO 300736  76 S.E.
On the N. edge of the wood is a possible *tumulus*.

584  SO 292730  76 S.E.
The *place-name* Kinsley Wood = Kinning's ley. The *track* which skirts the N. boundary of this wood, S.E. to Lee Cottage, and then N.E. (called Gypsy Lane or Priest's Lane) to the Church Field, (in which is the site of the Roman villa, S.W. of Stow) comes from the N.W. from the lost church at Goreham near Five Turnings (see record no. 527). The fork to the S. of the wood goes to the chapelry at Knighton.

585  SO  310733   76 S.E.

This is the Church Field (see record no. 584) S. of the site of the Roman villa, the plough continues to strike stonework. Some observers have thought it to be the site of an original church, or further Roman remains. Thorough excavation is thus desirable in the interests of local history.

586  SO  375767   77 N.W.

There is a possible *Deserted Mediaeval Village* around Cresswell Cottages.

587  SO  368757   77 N.W.

The area in which the school stands, surrounded by a ring of roads, is the site of the *village green*.

588  SO  374756   77 N.W.

12 *flints* were found in the S. half of this field, and also a fragment of a polished *stone celt*, by D. G. Bayliss.

589  SO  382757   77 N.W.

10 worked *flint flakes* were found in this field by D. G. Bayliss.

590  SO  386750   77 N.W.

This R.D.C. *boundary* was originally marked out in 1536.

591  SO  382747   77 N.W.

The *place-name* Adleymoor was Adlacton in Domesday ( = on the lake).

592  SO  367765   77 N.W.

The mound is a *tumulus* and not a motte, although its local name is 'Oval Mount'.

593  SO  371774   77 N.W.

This *earthwork* is 80 ft. in diameter with a 9 ft. vallum. The *field* in which it is sited is called Warfield. (the Anglo-Saxon word 'waru' = look-out).

594  SO  380777   77 N.W.

This *road* is probably *Roman* from Leintwardine to the lead mines at Shelve. Though marred by the railway at Hopton Heath, it passed S. to Heath Lodge, then S.E. by the footpath to Heath House and beyond to the E. at 389761.

595  SO  365764   77 N.W.

E. of the printed B.S. is a *mound* which may be a tumulus.

596  SO  345765   77 N.W.

The *place-name* Meer oak is derived from the Old English 'meare' = boundary.

597   SO 350750   77 N.W.
> The area S.E. of this point consists of very small fields, and is considered a *Celtic settlement*.

598   SO 360750   77 N.W.
> The *place-name* 'Chat' = battle, according to local antiquarian traditions.

599   SO 368757   77 N.W.
> S. from the school, where there is a boundary stone, the original *road* crossed the park through the printed 'B' and 'C' of Bedstone Court and down the line of trees to the bend in the present road.

600   SO 354771   77 N.W.
> In the *place-name* Titterhill, 'Tit' is derived from the Saxon Twt = lookout. Cf. Titterstone (near Ludlow) and Tatteridge, near Leintwardine.

601   SO 360764   77 N.W.
> Around the B.M. 817·3 a *flint flake* was found by D. G. Bayliss of Leintwardine on 21st February 1954.

602   SO 407757   77 N.E.
> A set of 6 *lynchets*, through which a later *hollow-way* has been cut, lies around this point; on the S.E. side of the site is a square flat 'earth platform' in fair condition.

603   SO 412754   77 N.E.
> This road, which goes N.E. to 436763, is possibly a *Roman road* from Leintwardine to Bromfield.

604   SO 416763   77 N.E.
> N. and S. of this point for 800 yds. E. of Mocktree Hays, the area had by September 1953 yielded 6 *flint flakes*; and at the grid reference point, many 16th C. *pottery sherds* were also found. This was probably a *squatter's settlement* or enclosure.

605   SO 422763   77 N.E.
> Just to the E. of the road, a *flint arrowhead* was found in 1935 by H. C. Jones (headmaster of Clungunford School).

606   SO 415761   77 N.E.
> On the limestone quarry face, 6 ft. above the present base of the cutting, were found the lower jawbone with teeth, and the broken tibia of a Roe Deer embedded in the tufa in either a *cave* recess or crevice, into which it had apparently fallen in ancient times.

607   SO 399748   77 N.E.
> In this field, D. G. Bayliss found the handle of a native pot (*Romano-*

*British urn*) in October 1953, as verified by the National Museum of Wales at Cardiff. He also found 2 *flint flakes*.

608  SO 403756  77 N.E.
A small section of the *Roman road* (Watling Street) was exposed in the orchard of Stormer Hall in June 1953 by D. G. Bayliss (which the author visited with him). It revealed a cobbled surface with traffic ruts of 5 ft. span indicating width of axle. The road surface is 6 ins. below the turf, and the depth of the cobble road material averaged one foot.

609  SO 408754  77 N.E.
In this field in 1953 was found a grey *flint flake*, and later 2 others were recovered.

610  SO 396769  77 N.E.
E. of the river, and S. for 500 yds., are 2 areas of *field strips*; the longer one N. to S. had 17 strips and the smaller one, 300 ft. square, had 6 strips E. of the bend in the river opposite the printed word 'tumulus'.

611  SO 400766  77 N.E.
The road which runs E. from Marlow, past Woodhead and Bryan's Cottage, is a Welsh *Cattle Drovers' road* to Bilston in Staffordshire.

612  SO 410775  77 N.E.
The three fields W. of Stocking Rough contained a set of 17 *field strips*.

613  SO 410777  77 N.E.
N. of the road, the field with the printed 600 ft. contour, and the adjoining part of the next field to the corner of the wood, contained a set of 8 *field strips*.

614  SO 390763  77 N.E.
Along with the hoard of Bronze spearheads recorded, was found a *Roman jar* with lath working round the body; it was 5⅜ inches high. Miss Overton of Leintwardine has one bronze spearhead which either came from Broadward or from the Walford Tump.

615  SO 389754  77 N.E.
This is possibly part of the ancillary *Roman road* N. to the lead mines at Shelve.

616  SO 400762  77 N.E.
Miss Lily F. Chitty claims that in 1927 she noted an unrecorded *tumulus* at this spot near to the hedge by the road.

617   SO 398769   77 N.E.
    The footpath due S. from the B.M. 459·56 to the spot-level 423 was formerly the original *road*.

618   SO 397770   77 N.E.
    Immediately W. of Lynches, is the probable site of the earlier Broadward *bridge*.

619   SO 394768   77 N.E.
    This is the centre point of an area (bounded by the river on the E.) of 700 to 800 ft. long by 600 ft. wide, within which lay the now *decayed hamlet* of Broadward, as given on the Clungunford Estate Map of 1805.

620   SO 394766   77 N.E.
    This so-called tumulus is probably a *motte*.

621   SO 393764   77 N.E.
    This so-called tumulus is more likely to be a *natural* flood *deposit*.

622   SO 356739   77 S.W.
    This is not a tumulus, as was once thought, but is a *ringed motte* (as amended on new O.S. editions) in the moat of which a *bill-head* of the Civil Wars was unearthed in 1952. The report is with Miss Lily F. Chitty, and the specimen was with D. G. Bayliss of Leintwardine.

623   SO 356738   77 S.W.
    About 100 ft. S. between the footpath and the river Redlake, is a dis-used sawmill which possibly occupied the site of the original *cornmill* associated with the motte.

624   SO 346740   77 S.W.
    5 *flints* have been found in this field.

625   SO 359728   77 S.W.
    The footpath S.S.E. across Brampton Bryan Park, E. of Park Cottage, was the original *road* S. of Bucknell.

626   SO 370722   77 S.W.
    An Elizabethan *groat* of 1568 was found here.

627   SO 372725   77 S.W.
    The alignment of fairly straight field boundaries, E. of the Rectory, represents the course of the earliest *road* E. from Brampton Bryan.

628   SO 385723   77 S.W.
    This *tumulus* is 18 yds. in diameter.

629 SO 372740   77 S.W.

St. James the Great *Church* is not old, but is, in fact, a small modern timber structure which has in recent years been removed bodily to Buckton at 384735 in the N. corner of the orchard.

630 SO 388743   77 S.W.

*Flints*, and especially *scrapers*, have been recovered from this field and the next one W.

631 SO 353739   77 S.W.

Between 100-200 *flints* have been found here, including a *petit tranchet arrowhead*.

The *place-name* Bucknell = Buchehelle (or Bucca's Hill), or it may be from O.E. 'bucca' = 'he-goat'.

632 SO 348741   77 S.W.

In the corner just E. of the ford, a *stone bowl* of natural concretion was found.

633 SO 355733   77 S.W.

In the middle of this field S. of the vicarage, have been found 300 pieces of *flint*. Miss Lily F. Chitty cannot recognise any implements; they probably represent the waste flint material from a chipping-floor. There is a significant *track* from this site going directly into the camp on Coxall Knoll.

634 SO 365730   77 S.W.

On the S. bank of the river, opposite New Park, is believed to be the site where Romano-British *potsherds* were found some years ago.

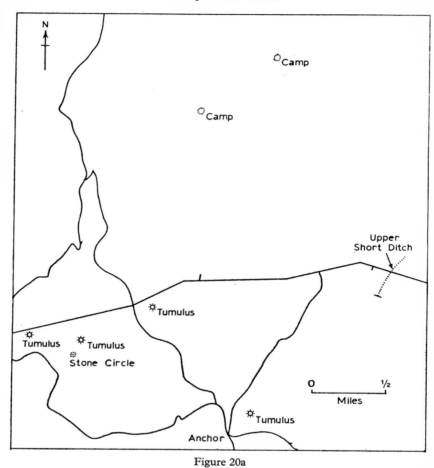

Figure 20a

Before fieldwork.
Sketch map of antiquities on O.S. sheet SO 18 (1963)

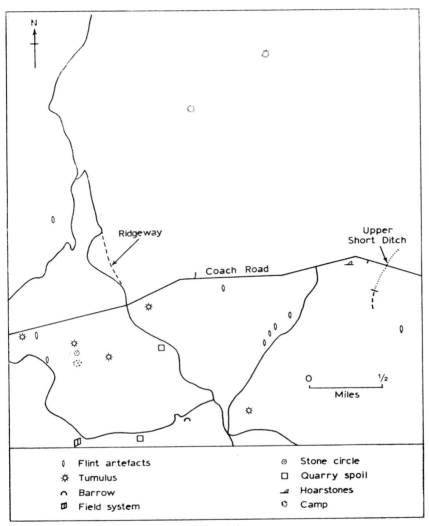

**N**

Ridgeway

Upper
Short Ditch

Coach Road

O _____ ½
Miles

| | Flint artefacts | | ⊕ | Stone circle |
| ☼ | Tumulus | | ☐ | Quarry spoil |
| ∩ | Barrow | | ◢ | Hoarstones |
| ▥ | Field system | | ◌ | Camp |

**Figure 20b.**

After fieldwork.
Showing additional sites on the same map.